LOST
TOWNS OF THE SWIFT RIVER VALLEY
DROWNED BY THE QUABBIN

Elena Palladino

THE
History
PRESS

Published by The History Press
Charleston, SC
www.historypress.com

Copyright © 2022 by Elena Palladino
All rights reserved

Back cover: Farewell Ball invitation image courtesy of Friends of Quabbin. Farewell Ball dancing photo courtesy of the Swift River Valley Historical Society.

First published 2022

Manufactured in the United States

ISBN 9781467147972

Library of Congress Control Number: 2022939452

Notice: The information in this book is true and complete to the best of our knowledge. It is offered without guarantee on the part of the author or The History Press. The author and The History Press disclaim all liability in connection with the use of this book.

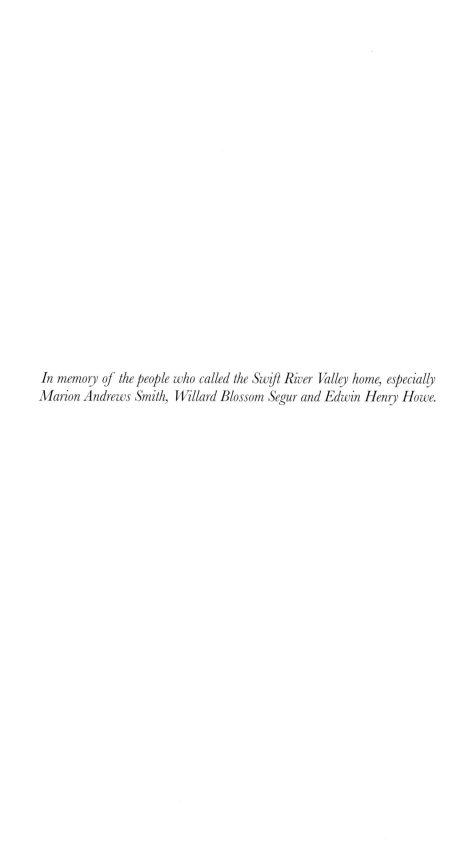

In memory of the people who called the Swift River Valley home, especially Marion Andrews Smith, Willard Blossom Segur and Edwin Henry Howe.

Contents

Contents

PREFACE

In the 1930s, four Massachusetts towns disappeared.

Boston needed drinking water, so the Commonwealth of Massachusetts disincorporated the central Massachusetts towns of Enfield, Greenwich, Dana and Prescott in order to create a massive reservoir in the bowl-shaped Swift River Valley. After the towns were legally dissolved in April 1938, they then physically disappeared, as the Swift River was dammed and the valley gradually filled with 412 billion gallons of water, all of it bound for the city of Boston and its neighbors. When it was completed in 1946, the Quabbin Reservoir was the largest man-made reservoir in the world and was heralded as an engineering marvel. Today, the Quabbin provides high-quality unfiltered water for over three million people in Boston and its surrounding towns.

But there was a human cost to the building of the Quabbin. Although the reservoir may have yielded the greatest good for the greatest number of Massachusetts residents, its construction fundamentally altered the lives of more than two thousand people. They were forced to leave their lifelong homes. Their land, houses and businesses were taken, emptied, razed and burned. The bodies of their lost loved ones were exhumed from local cemeteries and reinterred elsewhere. Some were resigned to their fate, and some were defiant, but all were heartsick to be made to leave and to see their homeland flooded with water for Boston.

My interest in this subject came about in a very personal way. In 2015, my husband, daughter and I moved into a Colonial Revival house in Ware.

We were intrigued to hear neighbors referring to our new home as the "Quabbin House" and learned that it had been built by a woman named Marion Andrews Smith when she was forced to leave Enfield, her lifelong home. Marion was the last surviving member of a prominent and wealthy industrialist family that had lived in Enfield for generations. Although we heard rumors that she had her whole house moved from Enfield, we soon found out that she in fact took parts of her Victorian house and had them built into her new house in Ware.

My curiosity about Marion really picked up speed in 2018. That fall, a mysterious envelope appeared in our mailbox. It contained two black-and-white photos of our house when it was newly completed in 1939. There was no writing on the photos or return address on the envelope, so we never knew who left it for us. But those photos started me on a quest, first to the Quabbin Visitor's Center, then to local archives like the Swift River Valley Historical Society and eventually on a search for a woman by the name of Marian Tryon Waydaka,[1] the daughter of Marion Smith's housekeeper and chauffeur, who had lived with Marion Smith until the early 1940s.

When I finally tracked down Marian Tryon Waydaka—by then nearing age ninety—she greatly enriched my understanding of the woman for whom she'd been named. In my research, Marion Smith came across as dignified, admirable and stoic, but the younger Marian's stories about her Nana brought her alive as a woman deeply involved in building her community and profoundly aggrieved by Boston's plans to destroy the Swift River Valley in order to a build a reservoir. Marion and her household members, including the young Marian Tryon, were among the very last to leave Enfield in the summer of 1938.

Perhaps inevitably, my research gradually expanded into a larger quest: to learn all I could about the people of the lost towns of the Swift River Valley, what their lives had been like and how and why the state forced them to leave. The final result is this book. The tale that unfolds in parts 1 and 3 focuses primarily on Enfield and its environs, in particular on three of its most prominent residents: Marion Andrews Smith, Willard "Doc" Segur and Edwin Henry Howe. Part 2 presents the other side of the story: Boston's centuries-long struggle to provide enough fresh water for an ever-growing populace and economy and why, to the powers that be, the building of the Quabbin appeared to be the ideal solution.

Those of us who are fortunate enough to call the Quabbin region home are well aware of the sacrifices made by former Swift River Valley residents. We also benefit from endless opportunities to engage with the natural beauty of the vast state lands that surround the Quabbin Reservoir today. But the reality is that the reservoir's appealing "accidental wilderness" is a result of artificially altered river flows and the dissolution of a two-hundred-year-old community. Beneath Quabbin's peaceful waters lies a homeland for many people that was taken forever.

My intention, in telling the stories of these people and the homeland they lost, is to honor their memories and their fates through a better understanding of how and why the Quabbin was built—and what was sacrificed for Boston in the name of progress.

OF COURSE, THE UPROOTED residents of Enfield, Greenwich, Dana and Prescott were not the first people driven from the valley by forces more powerful than they were. That tale is beyond the scope of this book, but I believe it is important to at least acknowledge it here.

Long before European settlers arrived, the Swift River Valley was home to the eastern Algonquin peoples: the Nipmuc, along with the neighboring Massachusett, Pequot, Pocumtac and Wampanoag tribes. The Nipmuc (an Algonquin word meaning "freshwater people") inhabited much of central Massachusetts, and their presence stretched as far south as northern Connecticut and Rhode Island. They called the Swift River Valley *Qaben*, meaning "the place of many waters." This name is also attributed to a Nipmuc sachem or chief whose tribe had a settlement where two branches of the Swift River met, the same location that much later became the site of Enfield.[2]

The Nipmucs' main livelihood consisted of hunting, gathering and fishing. Their social unit was the village, which was mobile and followed food supplies. Their economy was a seasonal one that made use of central Massachusetts's many freshwater lakes and rivers. They lived in portable *wetus*, or domed huts, at the edges of lakes and rivers and used birchbark canoes, nets and weirs (a type of trap and the namesake of the nearby town of Ware) to catch fish.

Dwelling inland, the Nipmuc were not the first Native New Englanders to encounter Europeans; the Wampanoag and Massachusett people to the east had earlier encountered French fur traders traveling south from what is now eastern Canada. Along with their goods, the traders brought infectious diseases that the Native people had no immunity to. Beginning with the first epidemic around 1616, plagues ravaged all Native tribes of New England in subsequent decades. By some calculations, the Indigenous population decreased by as much as 80 to 90 percent in a span of just fifty years—a staggering loss of life within one generation.[3]

While plagues decimated Native communities in the first half of the seventeenth century, King Philip's War further depleted them in the second half. In 1671, following the death of grand sachem Massasoit, who helped to keep the peace between Native people and colonists for many years, the southern New England tribes banded together under Massasoit's second son, Metacomet, also known as King Philip, in an effort to drive the English colonists out of New England. They attacked many of the sixty-four towns throughout the Massachusetts Bay Colony. In one battle, known as the Great Swamp Fight, in December 1675, it is estimated that more than six hundred Narragansett people were killed.[4]

King Philip's War was the deadliest war in American history per capita. Approximately one thousand colonists (and one in ten adult men of the Massachusetts Bay Colony) and more than three thousand Native people, including women and children, died between 1675 and 1678. In addition, over the course of the war, two-thirds of New England settlements were attacked and more than half destroyed. The economies of Plymouth and the Rhode Island colonies were devastated, and most white settlers were forced to retreat to the coastal colonies for a time.[5]

Fifty years later, in 1732, with the Native population significantly diminished, the Massachusetts Bay Colony gave land grants to encourage westward expansion and population growth. In a perverse twist of "ownership," the General Court of Massachusetts gave grants of central Massachusetts land to soldiers who fought in the Great Swamp Fight, the battle in which so many Narragansett people were killed. Within this "Narragansett Township" lay the Quabbin Parish, so named for the Nipmuc word for the area.

In later years, according to Quabbin settlers, many Native relics, such as arrowheads, stone bowls, pestles, hatchets and other "unique remains," were found by farmers plowing their fields, which were located "on the sites of ancient wigwams."[6] One relic reportedly found in the vicinity was the intact skeleton of a Native person buried in a sitting posture.[7] But while these remains attested to their former presence, by the time white settlers were repopulating this area, the Nipmuc were virtually gone, as were the Narragansett and other tribes. Mere traces of their existence remained to remind settlers of the people who had been there before them, whose land they had taken and whose population and communities they had decimated.

This was the first taking of Quabbin lands.

ACKNOWLEDGEMENTS

This book would not have been possible without the support and assistance of so many friends and colleagues.

First and foremost, I am indebted to the people who have researched and written about the history of the Swift River Valley and the Quabbin Reservoir before me, including Donald Howe, J.R. Greene, Elizabeth Peirce and Elisabeth Rosenberg. Howe's *The Lost Valley*, in particular, is a comprehensive catalog of the people, places and things that once made up the valley. Without this massive compilation of memories, genealogies and "quaint items," much more of the Swift River Valley's history would have been lost to time or would be less accessible than it is today. I also want to extend special thanks to Beth Rosenberg, who has been so generous with her time and her research. Thanks to Springfield historian Derek Strahan, who introduced me to The History Press.

Appreciation is also due to the local historical and cultural organizations that maintain the records of the Swift River Valley. The Swift River Valley Historical Society is an incredible archive and museum dedicated to the history of the Swift River Valley, and I am especially grateful to Dot Frye and Megan O'Loughlin, who were so kind, patient and helpful with my research. The Quabbin Visitor's Center includes a branch of the Massachusetts Department of Conservation and Recreation (DCR) and holds the Swift River Valley's vital records, along with the Quabbin's engineering and cemetery records. I owe a debt of gratitude to Nancy Huntington of DCR, who showed an interest in my research on Marion Smith since our very first meeting at the visitor's center in November 2018. Maria Beiter, also of DCR, has been a helpful guide and always quick to answer my (many) questions. Thanks to both Nancy and Maria for reading drafts of portions of this book. The Forbes Library in Northampton has wonderful scrapbooks compiled by Joseph Harrison, librarian from 1912 to 1950. Thanks to archivist Julie Bartlett Nelson for her assistance with the many photos from Forbes Library that appear in this book.

Thanks to Gene Theroux, president of Friends of Quabbin, and to Marty Howe and Jon Melick, who also read draft portions of this book. I highly recommend Marty and Jon's guided Quabbin hikes, which are offered by the Swift River Valley Historical Society. Appreciation is also due to Cynthia LaBombard, who shared her research on Doc Segur with me just months before her death in 2020.

Of course, this book would not have come into being without Marion Andrews Smith. Inhabiting her home has allowed me to inhabit her story, her life and her pain, and this book was written with love, admiration and sorrow for her.

I am grateful that my interest in Marion Smith led me to Marian Tryon Waydaka, who lived with Marion Smith until she was fourteen years old. Marian died in March 2021, before I could share this book with her. I am indebted to her son, Mark Waydaka, who shared Marian's papers with me as I was writing this book. To Mark and the Waydaka family, thank you. This book would not have been possible without your generosity. My gratitude also to Peter Howe; Donna Segur Marangoni and her husband, Alan; and Stephanie Hayward for speaking with me about the Howes and the Segurs.

Next, some personal dedications. I want to send love and thanks to those who helped and supported me along the way: Jenn Barnes, Ariel and Caleb Gannon, my aunt Tina and my best friend, Laura. I also want to thank my editor, Nancy Doherty, who helped me find my way through this story, in words and in confidence.

And finally, special acknowledgement goes to my family.

My dad, whose love of fishing the Quabbin meant the reservoir was familiar to me from a young age.

My mom, an excellent writer and genealogist whose appreciation of family history influenced my own. (And thanks for the childcare, too!)

My creative and talented brother, the first person to read my book proposal.

And most especially my husband, Matt, who convinced me we should buy Marion Smith's house in Ware and who gave me a copy of *The Lost Valley* for my birthday. Matt, you believed in this book long before I did, and you did everything you could to ensure I could start writing and keep writing, even during a pandemic. Thank you.

Last but not least, my incredible daughters. Evelyn, your excitement on the days I found time to write sometimes exceeded my own. Thank you for being my biggest cheerleader. And to my Marion: I finally "found" my book! And I hope you will always find inspiration in your namesake.

Prologue

THE FAREWELL BALL

When the sun began to set behind the round hills of the Swift River Valley in rural central Massachusetts, it usually signaled the start of a quiet night to come. But on the unseasonably warm spring evening of Wednesday, April 27, 1938, the few remaining Enfield residents hurried to finish their dinners and put on their Sunday best, while hundreds of out-of-towners poured into town in automobiles, causing a traffic jam on Main Street. The hopeful signs of spring in New England—flowering fruit trees, blooming tulips, the town hall decked out in bunting usually reserved for celebrations—had become harbingers instead of a funeral, the bunting edged in black for this last, mournful occasion.

Enfield—along with three other small towns: Greenwich, Prescott and Dana—were being sacrificed so that the Commonwealth of Massachusetts could build a massive reservoir to serve Boston and its surrounding towns. After decades of exponential population growth in the eastern part of the state, Boston turned its sights westward, toward the Swift River Valley, to satisfy its seemingly insatiable need for drinking water. Tonight's Farewell Ball constituted the final hours of Enfield's existence; midnight would toll the death knell of the Swift River Valley towns.

Valley residents had known for a little over a decade that this night would come—and there had been hints for decades before that—so many had planned their exits accordingly. Since 1927, when the state passed the Swift River Act, most people had sold their land to the state and left. But to a small segment of the residents, especially older folks whose families

Left: April 27, 1938: the Enfield town hall decorated for the Farewell Ball. *Swift River Valley Historical Society*.

Below: Enfield's town hall the night of the Farewell Ball. Photograph by Arthur Griffin, titled *7:30 p.m. Griffin Museum of Photography*.

Opposite: Portrait of Marion Andrews Smith in her younger years. *Tryon family collection*.

had lived in the valley for generations, the arrival of this day seemed impossible. And so they remained.

Nonetheless, in the coming months, their land would be taken, and they would be made to leave. By then, the town they loved and helped to build would be unrecognizable—fires were ablaze as the houses they grew up in and raised their own children in were burned, and all trees and vegetation were cut to the earth by young men nicknamed "woodpeckers." Already for months they had been subjected to the constant noise of the construction of the great dike and earthen dam rising at Enfield, "ominous sentinels of the valley's future."[8]

One of those lingering residents was Marion Andrews Smith. At seventy-six, she represented the third generation of the Smith family to live in Enfield and was its sole surviving member, now forced to leave against her will. Her younger brothers, Edward and Alfred, along with her mother, Loraine, her father, Henry, and her uncle Edward, had all died since the turn of the century, and Marion had recently faced the difficult task of deciding where to rebury them after their remains were exhumed from Enfield's Cemetery Hill Cemetery in anticipation of the reservoir.

The Smiths' house, a sixteen-room Victorian in the Queen Anne style built in 1896, was known as "the most impressive of all places, that big house on a knoll."[9] Located between Mount Ram and Little Quabbin, the house had views of the hills surrounding the valley on all sides, and the family chose to name it Bonnieview.

Marion was born in 1862, during the Civil War, and was called Minnie in her younger years. Her brother Alfred was born two years later and Edward nine years after that, in 1873. Those who knew Marion described her as "aristocratic" and "regal."[10] The child of a Swift River Manufacturing Company employee once said that around Miss Smith "you felt as though you had to say just the right thing and look just the right way."[11]

Marion attended Bradford Academy in Haverhill, at that time a private secondary school for women. Her activities were reported frequently in the society pages of the local papers, as she and her mother traveled together to such destinations as Atlantic City, Casco Bay in Maine and also Boston, for meetings of the Bradford Academy Club. By 1914, the Smith family owned

The Smith family home, Bonnieview. *Forbes Library's Quabbin Reservoir albums, compiled by Joseph Harrison.*

an automobile and newspapers began reporting whether they "motored" to their various destinations.

Marion came of age during a time of prosperity for Enfield and also during her father and uncle's successful leadership of the Swift River Manufacturing Company. The Smiths were very civic minded and generous with their time and wealth. This context and her upbringing shaped her own active approach to civic engagement. Marion became one of the first women to join the school committee, served as a charter member and first president of the Quabbin Club and was president of the Library Association, among many other social and civic commitments.

By 1938, Marion lived alone in the family home along with her hired help, the Tryons, who had become like family to her: Earl Tryon, the groundskeeper and chauffeur; Bridget "Delia" Tryon, the housekeeper and cook; eight-year-old Marian Agnes Tryon, Marion Smith's namesake, who called her Nana; and Delia's cousin Catherine "Kay" Sullivan, who assisted with housekeeping. As of the Farewell Ball, Marion and the Tryons still had not made plans to leave Enfield. Marion's friend Doc Segur told a local newspaper he feared Marion might not live even two months longer, because "her trouble is a broken heart."[12]

Left: Marion Smith in her later years at Bonnieview. *Tryon family collection.*

Right: Portrait of Willard "Doc" Segur in his younger years. *Personal collection of Willard Segur's granddaughter Donna Segur Marangoni.*

The Segur family home. *Metropolitan District Water Supply Commission (MDWSC) real estate photos, via Digital Commonwealth.*

LITTLE QUABBIN FROM RES. OF W.B.SEGUR,M.D,, ENFIELD,MASS.

View of Little Quabbin from the Segur family home. *Forbes Library's Quabbin Reservoir albums.*

Seventy-three-year-old Willard "Doc" Segur also remained in the valley with his wife, Laura, in a home on Bridge Street near the Swift River. Though not a town native, Doc had become an integral part of the community, even above and beyond his longtime profession as the valley's doctor.

Doc was known, above all, for his warm bedside manner and his "affable and kindly nature."[13] Born in Talmadge, Ohio, in 1865 to the Reverend Seth Willard and Ellen Blossom Segur, Doc attended Phillips Andover Academy in Massachusetts and then Princeton University, where he excelled as an athlete. In 1889, Doc entered Dartmouth Medical College in New Hampshire, where he played baseball and football and sang in the glee club. Before graduating in 1892, he composed Dartmouth's well-known and loved football standard, "As the Backs Go Tearing By."

Following a residency at Boston Emergency Hospital, Doc settled in Enfield in 1895 with his first wife, Mary, and their adopted son, Harold, and opened his practice on Main Street. Doc and Mary divorced in 1907. Two years later, he married Laura G. Warren Hageman of nearby Greenwich Village. They had one son, Willard "Bill" Segur Jr., born in 1912.

As a country doctor, Doc divided his time between seeing patients in the office and traveling to homes all over the Swift River Valley, first with his four horses pulling his carriage (or sleigh in the snowy winter months) and, after 1905, in his Dodge four-cylinder coupe.[14] Doc was well known for being

Top: Doc Segur in his later years. *Swift River Valley Historical Society.*

Bottom: Portrait of Edwin H. Howe circa 1900. *Personal collection of Edwin Howe's great-grandson Peter Howe.*

flexible in what he accepted as payment for his services, including goods, chickens, trout and garden produce. The many poor valley residents appreciated his generosity.

In addition, Doc Segur served as Enfield's school physician. He was known for his rapport with children as well as for his good humor. One story shared in a Springfield newspaper was about a young boy who, after getting a vaccination, nearly fainted in front of his classmates. Doc quickly said, "You know son, when I was vaccinated, I passed right out." The article asks, "Who was the hero then?"[15]

Doc served as the first chief of staff at Mary Lane Hospital in Ware and held most town offices at one point or another—he was a selectman for many years and served as chair of that board, and he also was chief of the volunteer fire department, town physician, school physician, head of the health board and medical examiner for the district. He also held other leadership positions in county offices and professional organizations.

Doc presided over the final town meeting on April 12, 1938, as chair of the board of selectmen. As fire chief, he chaired the planning committee for Enfield's Farewell Ball, which the Enfield Fire Department sponsored. At the ball, he and Laura led the grand march, and at the stroke of midnight, it was Doc who conducted the solemn moment of silence that marked the town's passing into history.

At age seventy-nine, Edwin Henry Howe was among the oldest Enfield residents, not only in years but also in family history. Edwin was born in Enfield in 1859 and attended nearby Wilbraham Academy before enrolling at the Eastman Business School in Poughkeepsie, New York. He

Left: Edwin Howe in his later years. Photograph by Arthur Griffin. *Griffin Museum of Photography.*

Below: The Howe family home. *Forbes Library's Quabbin Reservoir albums.*

Enfield

then returned to Enfield and, in 1887, became manager of the telephone exchange, located in the Howe homestead, and also served as postmaster for twenty-five years. With his son Ned, Edwin continued to maintain the post office at their general store on Main Street until near the end of Enfield's existence.

Like Doc, there was nothing Edwin and his sons Donald and Ned would not do for Enfield; Edwin served as deacon and trustee of the Congregational church, selectman, secretary of the Masonic Lodge (and recipient of its fifty-year medal after serving in every Masonic office), notary public, town clerk and member of the school board.

Marion, Doc and Edwin were among thousands who gathered in Enfield for the ball—the crowd that evening exceeded the size of the towns at their peaks. But unlike the former residents who returned for the evening, the curious onlookers or the young revelers, Marion, Doc and Edwin were honored guests, being the oldest generation of Enfield residents forced to say goodbye to their beloved homes and to the community they helped to build.

As they took their seats at the front of the ballroom and gazed at the black crepe streamers and bunting hanging from the town hall rafters, their thoughts might well have turned to an event they all attended there twenty-two years earlier—Enfield's Centennial, a hopeful celebration of the town's contributions to the world, when it still seemed possible that Enfield might continue to flourish in the coming decades. The centennial was celebrated over Fourth of July weekend in 1916, when the dark clouds of the reservoir had begun to gather but had not yet fully darkened the valley's skies.

PART I

THE SWIFT RIVER VALLEY— BEFORE

The cove of the Swift River at Enfield with Little Quabbin in the background. *Forbes Library's Quabbin Reservoir albums.*

MY HEART IS CLIMBING THE HILLS

By Charles E. Ewing, former pastor of the Congregational church
Written for Enfield's centennial, July 1916

One place in old Massachusetts
Is calling me now to come home—
Yes, home, the home of my childhood;
And since I have left it to roam
In many populous cities,

With houses and churches and mills,
While I am surrounded by people
My heart is climbing the hills.

In thought again I am climbing
The hills that we all used to climb;
In thought again I am walking
The paths of the boyhood time.
Amid the clash of loud voices
I hear just a whisper that thrills;
The whisper of Enfield is calling;
My heart is climbing her hills.

I crossed the distant Pacific;
I lived in the land of Cathay;
I saw the swift revolution,
The coming of China's new day.
I heard the cry of the millions
Who suffer beneath the world's ills;
But while I was far off from Enfield,
My heart was climbing her hills.

And now, I live in my homeland,
America, best in the world.
I wish I might be in Enfield;
Might there see the old flag unfurled;
Might there renew old friendships;
Might join in the games and the drills.
I live on the rolling prairie,
But my heart is climbing the hills.

The hundred years' celebration
Will welcome a home-coming throng.
And oh, that I might be with them,
To join in the greeting and song.
To visit the places that childhood
Still peoples, and memory fills;
My life may be lived on the lowland,
But my heart is climbing the hills.

Chapter 1

PLANNING THE CENTENNIAL

A ll roads lead to Enfield" was the slogan selected for Enfield's hundredth birthday celebration, a three-day affair held over Fourth of July weekend in 1916.[16] Though the town's actual incorporation took place on February 15, 1816, the centennial planning committee chose a summer weekend in the hopes of excellent weather, particularly for the many former residents who would be returning via automobile.[17] Traffic officers were stationed in the center of town to direct the influx of vehicles on the usually quiet streets, enabling Enfield to enjoy "the city dignity of street traffic for two days of her history."[18]

The centennial was more than six months in the making and was a true community effort, with many current and former residents providing financial support and joining the various planning committees. As the weekend approached, the town was decorated with patriotic bunting, flags and signs, "almost every building and residence bearing some emblem of patriotism."[19] A welcome sign was hung between two columns in the center of town and was lit up at night. The "Bonnieview block" of Smith's Village, the village of Enfield where the Smith's Swift River Manufacturing Company was located, was decorated, as were the Howe block on Main Street and many residences. More than eight thousand people attended the final day's festivities, which included the Fourth of July parade and fireworks. Even the clouds that began to gather on the second day of the celebration could not dampen Enfielders' pride in the town's distinguished past and their hopes for its future.

Enfield's Main Street decorated for the 1916 centennial. *University of Massachusetts's Special Collections and University Archives Enfield (Massachusetts) Collection.*

The centennial's executive committee consisted of five prominent Enfield men: Willard Segur, chairman; young Donald Howe, secretary; and Edwin H. Howe, Josiah Flint and Charles Felton, all of whom were selectmen. These men played key roles not only in planning the centennial but also in building the community that Enfield had cause to celebrate.

The executive committee convened eleven subcommittees that orchestrated every moment of the long weekend with a wide variety of events, including church services; historical sermons and dedications; concerts and parades; sporting events, including a road race and baseball games; and an old home day reception to welcome back former residents.

The town appropriated $400 in funds when the planning began in earnest in the winter of 1916 and also raised at least $600 from Enfielders. As resident H.E. Townsend wrote to the planning committee, "This is an affair which everybody in town should be proud and eager to push toward success. None too poor to participate, none too rich to evade, and if each contributes as he is able, then the credit should be equal."[20]

To this end, the executive committee also took volunteer recruitment for the event seriously. They engaged nearly seventy current and former Enfielders to join the planning effort on various subcommittees, including more than thirty women. This community effort was as significant an aspect of the event as the celebration itself, and the *Globe*'s headline about the centennial said that "everybody [is] working to make it a big success."[21]

Those who could not attend sent telegrams and letters to be read aloud, so their voices, at least, were present. In addition to these letters and many newspaper articles about the event, four texts from around the time of the centennial provide a sense of how Enfielders saw themselves and their town in 1916, particularly regarding the town's history and its residents' deeply held values of Puritanism and patriotism.

The first is the historical sermon the Reverend Frederick B. Richards gave at the opening anniversary service on Sunday, July 2, published in full over three pages in the *Springfield Republican* on July 3, which detailed Enfield's history and religious context. In addition, two historical works by women were published in a bound program for the centennial; a poem entitled "Lines on the One Hundredth Anniversary of Enfield Massachusetts" by Carrie Warren Harwood and "A Sketch of Enfield's History" by Amanda Woods Ewing. Finally, Enfield native Francis Henry Underwood's 1893 book *Quabbin: The Story of a Small Town with Outlooks upon Puritan Life,* which Richards praised in his sermon, presents an authoritative history of early Enfield. The following chapters use these texts, along with the timeline of the centennial events, to illuminate Enfield's storied past and hopeful future on the occasion of its one hundredth birthday.

Chapter 2

THE CHARACTER OF THE VALLEY

On Sunday, July 2, 1916, the sun shone down on Enfield as cool breezes blew through the rolling hills of the Swift River Valley. This first day of the town's centennial celebration began with an anniversary service in the Congregational church, a building constructed thirty years before the official incorporation of the town. The church stood on Enfield's Main Street, which ran parallel to the Swift River and alongside the tracks of the valley's Springfield, Athol and Northeastern Railroad, also known as the "Rabbit Run" or the "Soapstone Limited," located between the hills known as Great Quabbin and Mount Ram.

The hills surrounding the valley were quite distinctive and featured prominently in the town's appearance and identity. The church faced the tallest hill, known as Great Quabbin, which rose a thousand feet above sea level and five hundred feet above the valley floor. Francis Underwood called Great Quabbin "a delectable hill for children," whose summit offered views of "airy pastures, sparkling brook, and broad horizon." Across the river from Great Quabbin and behind the church loomed the rugged peak of Mount Ram, "a somewhat irregular but beautiful cone of granite, jagged here and there with projecting edges of rock" that "made an effective background for the white steeple" of the church. Finally, to the northeast, there was Little Quabbin, the least of the three hills, which "did its best in delaying the morning sun, in upholding the north end of summer rainbows, and in sending back reflections from its massy ledges at sunset."[22]

Town of Enfield from Great Quabbin with Mount Ram in the background. Congregational church on far left. *Forbes Library's Quabbin Reservoir albums.*

The valley's hills were the remains of a massive mountain range created 350 million years ago by the Acadian Orogeny, the collision of the landmasses of Africa and North America. In the more recent past, approximately 11,000 years ago, glaciers scooped out the Swift River Valley, leaving the riverbeds of the three branches of the Swift River and the hills of malleable rock that formed the valley's perimeter and the sixty hills within.[23] Many of the hills are long, unevenly shaped masses known as drumlins, stretching in the direction of glacial movement; however, some of the peaks have the unusual look of miniature mountains, with steeper grades and distinct summits.

A sunny July day would have found Enfield's natural beauty on display and the air redolent of the valley's young forests, "a fresh, cheery smell, that is partly earthy, and partly leafy."[24] If not for the big event, children might have been "climbing up the rocky steeps of Mt. Ram," feeling "the lure of the old swimming hole" or enjoying "the delights of boating on the river."[25] Instead, many of the town's eight hundred residents were gathered in the Congregational church on this summer morning, the interior of which was decorated with fragrant pink and white peonies for the occasion.[26] The church exterior, the only prominent Enfield building not decorated for the

Exterior of the Congregational church with the Soldiers' Monument in the foreground. *Forbes Library's Quabbin Reservoir albums.*

centennial, stood "severe in its simplicity and imposing in its solitary location above the street, at the very base of towering Quabbin."[27]

The pastor, the Reverend George R. Hewitt, welcomed the congregation and said it was fitting that the centennial should begin on a Sunday, "the Lord's day, as those who founded the town believed in God."[28] The first Quabbin settlers were mostly Calvinist Scots from Ulster—Puritans who sought to cleanse the church by doing away with the rituals and ceremonies too closely associated with Catholicism because they believed those practices were not rooted in the Bible.

Hewitt read from Deuteronomy 28, which outlines the blessings that will be received for obedience to God. In the King James Bible, the passage states, "If thou shalt hearken diligently unto the voice of the Lord thy God, to observe and to do all his commandments…the Lord thy God will set thee on high above all nations of the earth." It goes on to say that crops, livestock and barns will all be blessed "in the land he swore to your ancestors to give you."

The Puritans who settled the Massachusetts Bay Colony believed that the "new world," like God's gift of the promised land to the Israelites of the Old Testament, was their gift from God for their faithfulness and obedience to his laws. This belief in their divine right to the land, which was granted by God's will, served as the justification for their settlement of the land and also for the displacement of Native people who had lived in the area.

At the end of Hewitt's reading of Deuteronomy and discussion of God's gift of the Swift River Valley to the Puritan settlers, the Reverend Frederick B. Richards of St. Johnsbury, Vermont, a sixth-generation descendent of the early residents of Enfield, preached the historical sermon. Richards opened with Psalm 143:5: "I remember the days of old. I meditate on all thy works; I muse on the work of thy hands."

Richards said the desire to spend time remembering the past is both a "natural instinct" and a "strong fascination." He discussed the concepts of history and heritage and how those aspects of the past control each person's future—how they form and inform each individual's personality, social standards, influences, ideals, motives and even creativity. Likewise, he believed that every town and city developed a life of its own that could be traced back to its unique heritage, including its moral and spiritual origins, and that each town, like each individual, is an "accumulated product of the past."

Enfield's past was inseparable from the history of the rest of the valley. As Elisabeth Rosenberg notes in her book *Before the Flood*, the terms "Swift River Valley," "Quabbin" and "Enfield" were used interchangeably since Enfield's inception. The land that Native people first called Quabbin, the colonists officially named Quabbin on January 14, 1736. This was the day the general court formally granted the twelve hundred acres of the Quabbin Township to twelve men—they received fifty acres each for a house lot; the remaining acres were for a "general division" or town center—with the condition that each man would live there for at least four years, farm at least ten acres and reserve some acreage for a minister's home, schools, a burial ground and a meetinghouse or church.[29]

Such arrangements were common at the time and are the reason many Massachusetts towns are centered around a town common or village green, surrounded by a meetinghouse, a Congregational church, a cemetery and livestock grazing areas. Quabbin was incorporated as a parish in June 1749, then as a town in April 1754. When it became a town, its name was changed to Greenwich for the Duke of Greenwich of Scotland, which reflects the Scottish ancestry of many of the settlers.[30]

Many early Massachusetts townships like Greenwich were formed with large tracts of land. As villages on the outskirts of town became more populous, they would break away to form new towns and take portions of the original township's land with them. This was true of Greenwich, whose acreage was reduced in subsequent decades to form the towns of Enfield and Dana.

After its incorporation, three separate villages began to take shape in Greenwich—Greenwich Village, Greenwich Plains and the South Parish. Greenwich Village was the largest settlement, situated on the east branch of the Swift River near Mount Lizzie and Mount Pomeroy, hills named for settlers who were said to have been kidnapped and killed by Native people. Greenwich Plains was further south, named for its flat and fertile lands.

Greenwich

Greenwich Plains Church with Mount Pomeroy in the background. *Forbes Library's Quabbin Reservoir albums.*

The South Parish emerged seven miles below Greenwich Village at the convergence of the east and middle branches of the Swift River, where the Nipmuc people once had their settlement. South Parish residents felt it took too long to travel seven miles north to church and town, so in 1816, the South Parish separated from Greenwich and was incorporated as the town of Enfield, named for Robert Field, an early settler and prominent citizen. While Greenwich's economy remained primarily agricultural, Enfield's focused on the manufacturing made possible by the power of the Swift River. Several factories sprang up during the 1800s, including manufacturers of textiles and other materials. For this reason, Enfield became not only the largest but also the most prosperous of the four valley towns.

Two other valley towns were established around the same time—Dana in 1801 and Prescott in 1822. Much like Enfield, Dana was incorporated using tracts of Greenwich's and neighboring town Petersham's land. The town was named for Judge Francis Dana, who did much of the legal work to separate the new township from the established ones. Dana also had several villages, including North Dana, Dana Center and a village named for a large family, the Doubledays. It was once known as the "hat town," because one factory produced Shaker hoods and palm leaf hats. Other industries included a box factory and a soapstone quarry.

Like Enfield and Dana, Prescott was formed as a small parish with land from neighboring Pelham and New Salem and was named for William Prescott, a colonel who led troops in the Battle of Bunker Hill during the Revolutionary War. Prescott sat in the northeast corner of the Swift River Valley within Hampshire County, and its rocky soil challenged the farmers who settled there. Given its diffuse acreage, the town spawned many villages, including Prescott Center, North Prescott, Atkinson Hollow and Pelham Hollow (also known as Bobbinville for its bobbin factory). Prescott was also the location of the valley's one cultural landmark, Conkey Tavern.

Founded by the three McConkey brothers, Conkey Tavern was where Revolutionary War veteran and farmer Daniel Shays planned a key event of Shays's Rebellion. The rebellion was an uprising of central and western Massachusetts farmers and veterans against Boston's onerous economic policies. Enacted to ensure timely payment of taxes, these laws resulted in property foreclosures and arrests of rural farmers who had no financial means in the wake of the Revolutionary War.

After the rebels incited several incidents, including blocking judges from entering courthouses and preventing tax collectors from collecting from rural workers, Governor James Bowdoin convened a privately funded militia to suppress the rebels. In January 1787, when Shays and others led more than a thousand men to Springfield to raid the federal arsenal to procure weapons, the militia fired on them. Three of Shays's men were killed and twenty injured before they fled the scene. Following this debacle, the rebels retreated to nearby Chicopee, and Shays eventually fled to Vermont.

Shays's Rebellion is said to have influenced George Washington to strengthen the federal government. Under the 1777 Articles of Confederation, Congress had little power to take actions like funding troops or regulating commerce. Washington and other nationalists like Alexander Hamilton and James Madison began to advocate for a stronger national government capable of quelling such uprisings in the future. Ultimately, this led to the signing of the United States Constitution in September 1787, which established the federal government and its foundational laws.

Interestingly, neither the centennial texts nor Underwood's book associate Shays's Rebellion with Enfield or the Swift River Valley. Perhaps this is because Daniel Shays is more closely linked to the Connecticut River Valley (often called the Pioneer Valley), because he lived in Pelham during the rebellion; Pelham is a hill town that borders the Quabbin to the west but is more closely associated with Amherst and the Pioneer Valley than the Swift River Valley.

Though the valleys share a ridgeline to the east of the Connecticut Valley and to the west of the Swift River Valley, they are seen as distinctly different. Underwood suggests that only after the "rich alluvial lands" of the Connecticut Valley were settled was there any thought of occupying the nearby "narrow, wet [Swift River] valley, and the ragged knolls that enclosed it."[31] In *Before the Flood*, Rosenberg also makes this distinction, calling the Connecticut Valley "broad and fertile," while the Swift River Valley's defining characteristics are that it is "narrow, and lay in shadow."[32]

The Swift River Valley's rugged terrain factored prominently in early settlers' sense of themselves and their land. In her historical sketch, Ewing highlights the hardiness of the people who first settled the Quabbin Township: "The hilly country appealed to them and the journey being made on horseback for the most part, the absence of state roads, or indeed any roads at all did not disturb them." She goes on to say that "no less than ten families were located on Mount Quabbin despite the fact that bears were numerous and the silence of the night was not infrequently broken by the howling of nearby wolves."[33]

As Ewing mentions, state roads did not exist in the valley until after 1750. The "roads" that first existed in the Massachusetts Bay Colony were the paths made by Native people. The colonial settlers widened and cleared many of these paths for travel by horseback, then by cart and coach and finally by automobile. The early roads were maintained by the residents whose property they passed through, and they were quite rough and wild, especially at night. In *Historic Hampshire in the Connecticut Valley*, Clifton Johnson describes an Enfield pioneer who was attacked by a pack of wolves, which he fought off with an axe, on his return journey to Enfield from Northampton. Other wildlife was plentiful, and settlers worked to reduce the animals' numbers. Johnson reported that bears were so numerous that a settler "caught enough one fall to buy a yoke of oxen."[34] In 1797, a bounty of two dollars was offered for each wildcat killed in Greenwich.[35]

The first public highway outside of the valley, from Pelham to Chicopee, was built in 1764, followed by others that intersected the valley from Palmer to Greenwich and from Belchertown to Hardwick. In 1800, a toll road, the Sixth Massachusetts Turnpike, was constructed through the valley at a cost of $760 per mile, stretching forty-three miles from Amherst to Shrewsbury.[36] Others followed, including the Belchertown to Greenwich route in 1803 and the Petersham to Monson route in 1804. In 1835, the maintenance of many of these privately owned and operated turnpikes was turned over to the municipalities through which they had been built; by 1870, towns were collecting taxes to pay for highway maintenance and other town infrastructure. Enfield was also a stop on the Northampton to Boston stagecoach route, and coaches arrived every other day, announced by a horn that sounded throughout the valley.[37]

These elements of the early Quabbin Township—the ruggedness of its hills, the proliferation of its wildlife and the lack of well-maintained roads—made up the foundational folklore that defined Enfield's history and identity, its "accumulated product of the past," as Reverend Richards would put it. Enfielders saw themselves as rugged, independent, hearty and brave, having descended from individuals who settled the difficult terrain of the Swift River Valley and did so successfully.

These secular characteristics cannot be separated from the religious identity that defined Puritanism more broadly. Underwood says that Quabbin settlers possessed the Puritan values of "serious views, self-denial and determination."[38] And Richards suggested that those values had a "large constructive significance in building our early institutions and in molding our national life." Because early Massachusetts townships were required to build a church and employ a minister, towns and parishes formed a single entity, with no separation between religious and civic life; for this reason, Puritan values were core values for early Enfielders.

Enfield's Congregational church was built in 1786–87 when Enfield was still the southernmost parish of Greenwich. The church originally faced Mount Ram and was a "dingy sulphur color, and without a steeple."[39] The building underwent many reconstructions and improvements throughout the next century, including turning the entrance so the church faced Main Street in 1814,[40] adding a steeple with a bell inside and a gilded weathervane atop it and painting the building white with green shutters and trim. Inside, the pulpit stood above the square, uncushioned pews, which faced inward upon each other as a gallery. The church also had an organ and was known for its music, which some said was the finest in the state of Massachusetts outside of Boston.

Underwood structures his history of Enfield around the tenures of its ministers, whose terms of service were long and influential. Likewise, Richards commended Enfield's congregation for the longevity of its pastorates, noting that fifteen pastors had served the church since 1789, and the first four of those served for seventy-two years in total, an average of eighteen years each. The first and perhaps most notable was the Reverend Joshua Crosby, who served fifty years, from 1789 until 1838. Crosby served in the Revolutionary War and was also a chaplain in the War of 1812. He was known as a "vigorous sermonizer" and also a "prudent, kind and just" minister.[41]

While the puritan spirit of Quabbin's founders was originally an expression of intense earnestness and devotion, Richards said that same ethos later became associated with a "loveless, harsh and narrow attitude and spirit, which repressed and repelled, but could not inspire." Referencing changes brought about by the Great Awakening and other religious movements of the eighteenth and nineteenth centuries, he said that in 1916, the centennial congregation was fortunate "to live in a day when the Christian world has become more truly Christian in its conceptions of truth," drawing more from the New Testament than the Old. Richards said that because all denominations now came "together on the basis of Christian ideals of service, and in harmony with the spirit of the universal Christ," Enfielders had therefore deepened their original Christian values and faith.

Almost certainly sitting among that centennial congregation in 1916 were Marion Smith and Edwin Howe, both of whom had served as elected trustees of the Congregational church for a decade and would continue

The Swift River Valley—Before

in those roles for two decades more. In the nineteenth century, church membership was around 300 members each year, with an average of 100 members attending the annual and special meetings. Around 1850, when Enfield's population was just over 1,000 residents, the Congregational church membership accounted for at least 25 percent of the town's population. In 1916, when Enfield's population was around 800 residents, 196 of those were members of the Congregational church.[42] The other, smaller religious institution in Enfield was the Methodist church, founded in 1835; Enfield Catholics would attend services in the town hall, performed by priests from neighboring Ware.[43]

The Congregational church's Woman's Missionary Society had ties to the larger missionary movement in the United States, including the American Missionary Society and the Massachusetts Woman's Home Missionary Association. Both were Protestant-affiliated groups focused on promoting equality and spreading Christian values within the United States and abroad. The organizations played key roles during the Reconstruction era in the United States, helping to establish schools and colleges for formerly enslaved people in the South.

Enfield's Woman's Missionary Society was formed in February 1885 by fourteen women of the Congregational church, with Marion Andrews Smith serving as the first secretary and treasurer. The society discussed a range of subjects at its meetings. Domestic topics included its work on behalf of historically Black schools like Tuskegee and Fiske Universities in Alabama and Tennessee, respectively, and the Snow Hill Normal and Industrial Institute in Alabama. International topics included Japanese life and missions, "the country 'Siam,'" and "western women in eastern lands."[44] Marion and her mother, Loraine, served as delegates to the home missionary association and ladies missionary societies, often attending gatherings of those groups held in Boston and Springfield.

Marion and Edwin were also active on Enfield's school board in their efforts to improve the town's schools. In his sermon, Richards said that in Enfield, "respect for education and ambition to secure it have never been lacking" and that "the proximity of important schools and colleges has constantly allured a goodly number of our boys and girls to the paths of higher education, and many have thus been fitted for lives of larger usefulness both at home and in the broader field of the outside world." Likewise, in her historical sketch, Ewing notes that students from Enfield went on to study at Yale, Amherst, Vassar, Mount Holyoke, Smith and other institutions of higher education, many of which were not far away.

Exterior of Enfield's town hall, circa 1900. *Forbes Library's Quabbin Reservoir albums.*

Enfield's town hall on Memorial Day, circa 1900. *Forbes Library's Quabbin Reservoir albums.*

The South Parish's first school committee was formed in January 1759, and the first schoolhouse was built in 1765. In the late 1870s, Enfield was divided into eight school districts, and each district had its own single-room schoolhouse. All grades were often taught by just one teacher. When the Enfield town hall was built in 1884, it housed primary and grammar school rooms along with the selectmen's offices, an auditorium, a "lockup" in the basement and the town library.[45]

In 1899, a more modern grammar school was built next to the town hall, and its first principal was hired shortly thereafter. For a time, around the turn of the century, the town offered high school classes, but they were soon discontinued, and children attended high school in neighboring towns, most notably Belchertown and Athol, located south and north of the valley, respectively.

Initially, Enfield's school committee had nine members, but it was eventually consolidated to three. Edwin Howe served on the school committee for several years around 1889 and met his wife, Annie, a teacher, through his service. In 1891, Marion Smith became one of the first women on the school committee, along with her friend Amanda Ewing, author of the centennial historical sketch.

Like Marion, Amanda was a prominent figure in town. She was a member of the Woods family, one of Enfield's oldest. After graduating from Vassar College in 1870, she traveled the world with her husband, George C. Ewing. She and George returned to Enfield in 1884, where George's brother Edward was the minister of the Congregational church. Amanda was active in the church, serving as trustee, superintendent of the Sunday school and member of the Woman's Missionary Society and the Woman's Auxiliary. She also served as charter member of the Quabbin Club and as the first woman president of Enfield's Library Association in 1907. Following Amanda's pathbreaking service, Marion's mother, Loraine, served as president beginning in 1909, and then Marion assumed the same position in 1911 and held it for many years.

Enfield's Free Library Association was founded in 1881 and moved into the town hall after it was built. In 1916, Marion wrote in the library association's annual report that "the directors are glad to report an increasing patronage of the library each year, which tells them there is a growing desire for good reading by the people of the town."[46] Though the library room in the town hall was becoming too small for the town's needs, the library never moved from that building.

During their school committee service, Marion and Amanda played a significant role in raising the standards of the eight grammar schools and also in setting up an intermediate school in 1891.[47] The committee reported in 1892 that the intermediate school, "which started as an experiment, has proved itself a successful and necessary measure," because in one year the number of students enrolled at it had nearly doubled. The committee expected that by keeping students in the intermediate school at least two years, it would "materially raise the standard of the Grammar schools" as well. Another notable change during Marion and Amanda's tenure was the reporting of the gender breakdown of the number of pupils each year; during their years of service, the number of enrolled female pupils increased significantly.[48]

The prevailing message of many school committee reports was just how important an education, even grammar school alone, would be to the future citizens of Enfield and of America more broadly. In 1891, Marion and Amanda's first school committee report stated, "In order to have good towns and cities we must have intelligent, law-abiding people, and the more public spirited and patriotic men and women there are the better." Twenty-five years later, in 1916, Doc Segur sounded the same theme when he was chairman of the school committee and kindly requested "the sincere co-operation of parents with the teachers and committee" in order "to bring the schools up to the highest efficiency in preparing the children of today to become able citizens in the future."[49]

THE FIRST DAY OF the centennial celebration concluded as it began, in the Congregational church, with a vesper service. Reverend Richards also read letters by former residents who could not attend, including the poem at the beginning of this chapter, "My Heart Is Climbing the Hills" by Charles Ewing of Janesville, Wisconsin, who was Amanda's nephew and the son of former Congregational church pastor the Reverend Edward Ewing. With its descriptions of childhood memories amid Enfield's hills, Ewing's poem illustrated the quote on the centennial invitation, "How dear to my heart are the scenes of my childhood," printed beneath a photo of Enfield nestled among its hills.

Finally, Richards read a letter from Rear Admiral Austin M. Knight of Newport, Rhode Island, which said:

Although I have not seen it for more than thirty years, I can still call up a restful vision of [Enfield's] *shady streets and quiet homes with their atmosphere of simple dignity and prosperity. No doubt it has changed much since then, but I am sure that it still stands for the best traditions of New England town and country life, and that however much it may have prospered it has not grown away from the spirit of kindly and generous hospitality.*

And with this noble vision of their town in the minds of its residents, the first day of the centennial came to a close.

Chapter 3

HONORING ENFIELD'S FINEST

When day broke on Monday, July 3, the sky over Enfield was gray. Thunderstorms had rolled through overnight, and more rain threatened for the afternoon.

The centennial's second day began with a concert by the Greenfield Military Band and included baseball games against Amherst and Ware. Enfield lost both games.

The day's main event took place at one o'clock, as a marching band made its way down Main Street and came to a stop at the Civil War Soldiers' Memorial on the common in front of the Congregational church. The monument had been donated by the local Grand Army of the Republic (GAR) post and the Town of Enfield years earlier but, due to an irregularity in the site title, had never been dedicated.[50] Now GAR representatives were ready to honor the Enfield men who had fought in the nation's bloodiest and most significant conflict to date.

The monument featured a bronze soldier dressed in the Union uniform atop a Quincy granite pedestal. The soldier gazed off into the distance, holding his musket barrel in both hands, its back end resting on the ground. Bronze plaques on the four sides of the pedestal base commemorated the 107 Enfield men who fought in the Civil War. Nearby, closer to Main Street, a Confederate cannon and cannon balls were placed, also donated by the GAR.

At the conclusion of the parade, Commander Edwin H. Moore of the General William S. Lincoln GAR Post in Enfield welcomed the crowd. Moore was a leader among the active veterans in town, having served as a private in the Thirty-Fourth Massachusetts Infantry at Worcester during the Civil War. Among his war stories were those of being captured briefly at Shenandoah and later witnessing the surrender by General Lee in Virginia.[51]

Moore stood above the crowd on a stage draped with red, white and blue cloth, holding a small book in his hands as he made his remarks. Musical selections from the Henschel Male Quartet were interspersed with his speech, as were greetings from the senior vice-commander of the GAR, Daniel E. Denny of Worcester. Following Moore's dedication to "those who fought and fell in defense of their country,"[52] he introduced A.S. Roe, a past commander of the Massachusetts Department of the GAR.

Just then the skies opened, and the rain began to pelt down. The Boston papers reported that over an inch of rain fell in just thirty minutes in the eastern part of the state; so much that Boston's sewers flooded, and travelers were temporarily stranded.[53] In Enfield, the ceremony came to an abrupt stop while the crowd fled to the cover of the church for the remainder of the exercises.[54]

Once within the shelter of the church, Roe began his remarks, which focused on the abundance of Civil War memorials in Massachusetts. He said the commonwealth had more Civil War memorials than any other state in the Union—at least one per municipality—and speculated that the aggregate value of such monuments "runs well into the millions" of dollars.[55] Roe also praised the "war-spirit" of Enfield and all Massachusetts towns, which Underwood calls the "tenacity of patriotism."[56]

Richards touched on this point as well in his sermon, declaring that more than one hundred Enfield men enlisted to make "the great sacrifice of patriotism," an extraordinary number when one realizes that the town's population was never far above one thousand residents—and only about half of those men returned home. In speaking about Enfield's sons and daughters going on to lead useful lives in the wider world, Richards cited the town's military volunteers as chief among those pursuing useful and noble callings. In Ewing's estimation, the town's record in the Civil War "reflects only honor upon itself: men and money were both forthcoming and generously supplied to fill the ranks of the army and to meet the necessary requirements of the war."[57]

When not fighting for their country, Enfielders were working. Underwood observes that Enfield residents' commitment to the concept of work in general was "as unconsidered as air, yet as vital."[58] In addition to the fertile soil that enabled Quabbin residents to farm, the Swift River provided the waterpower for manufacturing, an industry that had employed hundreds of residents in various mills and factories since the eighteenth century. For example, from 1790 to 1820, there was a business that exported Quabbin whetstones from the sandstone formation of Great Quabbin Mountain; other Quabbin mills included a sawmill, a linseed oil mill, a boot and shoe manufacturer, distilleries and factories that made cut nails, pearl buttons from oyster shells and shoe pegs from birchwood.

However, Enfield's chief sources of income were two textile mills known as the Swift River Manufacturing Company and the Minot Manufacturing Company. The Minot Company was in Enfield Center, while the Swift River Company was located in a small village a mile north of town known as Smith's. Both mills thrived during the nineteenth century, experiencing decline in later years as a result of changing methods of manufacturing and greater competition from larger mills.

The factory that eventually became known as the Minot Company in 1837 began doing business in 1825, when a dam was built on the Swift River. When the wooden facility burned down in 1830, it was rebuilt as a stone structure. The company made satinets—fabrics made of cotton fiber with a satin-like finish—and later, Shaker flannels and lightweight cassimeres, fine, twilled woolen fabrics, sometimes blended with silk and used to make men's suits.

Smith's Village, looking northeast up the Swift River Valley, with Greenwich plains in the distance. *Forbes Library's Quabbin Reservoir albums.*

Swift River Manufacturing Company. *Forbes Library's Quabbin Reservoir albums.*

The larger and more successful mill, the Swift River Manufacturing Company, was founded in 1823 by David Smith from the nearby town of Granby. In 1845, David sold interest in the operation to his brother Alvin, and by 1852, their brother Edward had joined the enterprise as well. Prior to Edward's arrival, the mill made satinets along with cotton warp, a wide yarn used in weaving cotton fabric on looms. But soon after Edward joined the operation in 1852, the mill changed its production to "fancy cassimeres" on its thirty-five broad looms.

The Swift River Company's reputation flourished and became synonymous with the highest-quality woolen fabrics. In 1908, the *Ware River News* reported that Swift River Company fabrics could be found all over the United States and that the company

> *has always done business on the most strict principles and has been met with uncommon success, as it has always adhered to making only the best and when the Swift River company's goods are placed before the buyer there is no question in his mind as to what he will get, as their reputation has always been at the highest regard.*[59]

At the height of production in the mid-nineteenth century, the mill employed over 125 people—approximately one-tenth of Enfield's population—nearly all from Northern Ireland. Situated on four acres, with many outbuildings, the mill was operated by steam power and waterpower from the Swift River. Smith's Village also had a general store and post office established by Marion's uncle Edward Payson in 1891 and later operated by Marion's brother Alfred Waldo, who was elected postmaster in 1892. In addition, Smith's had a school, housing for workers and a station on the railroad that was built through the valley in the 1870s.

The Smiths no doubt supported the construction of this north–south Athol to Springfield railroad, which linked the Swift River Valley to the state's primarily east–west railway systems that ran north and south of the valley, especially the Boston & Maine and Boston & Albany lines. However, the valley railroad's construction was not without difficulty, and in the process, many valley residents suffered substantial financial losses, being so eager to connect the valley to the world that they purchased large amounts of stock in volatile companies that changed hands rapidly and under questionable circumstances.

In 1869, the Athol & Enfield Railroad Company was incorporated and authorized to build a railway from Athol to Belchertown; in 1872, the line was approved to extend further southwest to connect to Springfield, the largest city in western Massachusetts. In 1873, the year the railway opened, it was acquired by the Springfield, Athol & Northeastern Railroad Company, which was later acquired by the Springfield & Northeastern Railroad in 1878. Finally, in 1880, the line was purchased by the Boston & Albany Railroad, which leased it to the New York Central Lines beginning in 1900.

Howe and other historians report that many valley residents suffered financial loss in these transfers of ownership, as the bonds of Athol & Enfield and subsequent companies became worthless and the changes of railway ownership were on paper only, undertaken by the "numerous and pitiless"[60] robber barons of the late nineteenth century who sought "to squeeze every penny possible out of stockholders."[61] What's more, the railroad never paid the dividends promised at its inception and, in fact, operated at a loss.[62]

Nonetheless, when the railway opened on December 3, 1873, it had nineteen stations throughout its forty-seven miles of track, including stops at New Salem, North Dana, Greenwich Village, Greenwich, Smith's and Enfield. Because of these many stops—Howe reported that the train was "widely heralded as the 'stoppingest' train in a fifty-mile run in the nation"[63]—the train was affectionately called the Rabbit Run. It was

The "Soapstone Limited" train. *Forbes Library's Quabbin Reservoir albums.*

also known as the Soapstone Limited, for its journey past the soapstone quarries of Dana.

The veteran railroad conductor of the Soapstone Limited, Albert G. Bennett, was well liked and known to be quite accommodating to valley residents who were boarding and exiting the train. He would reportedly wait several minutes for farmers who were horse trading to board or would let people disembark at their houses, even when they were not near to a station. Bennett was known to say that it took more time to make all the stops than to make the journey itself, yet he still maintained a reputation for timeliness.[64]

Thus, the nearly fifty miles of the Soapstone Limited's track joined the 250,000 miles of railway track that Richards noted had been laid throughout the United States by 1916, which increased the speed of transportation and also increased the profitability of manufacturing in the United States. Manufacturing in Enfield reached peak production just after the railroad's completion, around 1875, when the total profits of the town's businesses were around half a million dollars.[65]

When the elder Edward Smith died in 1891 at eighty-six, his sons, Edward Payson and Henry Martyn, took over the Swift River Company. Like their father and uncles, the brothers enjoyed a positive reputation, known for their carefully kept facilities, their personal relationships with their workers and

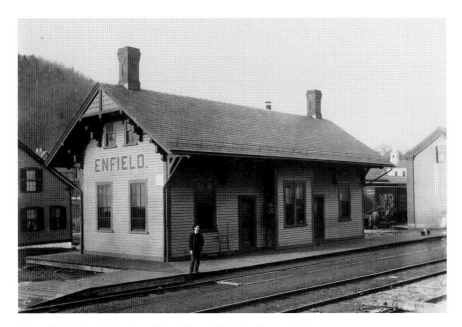

Above: Enfield's train station. *Forbes Library's Quabbin Reservoir albums.*

Opposite: Building the new steel railroad bridge across the Swift River, circa 1900. *Forbes Library's Quabbin Reservoir albums.*

their interest in the welfare of Enfield. Both brothers were active in civic affairs, with Henry serving as selectman in 1864 and Edward serving in the same role in 1866. Edward also represented the town in the legislature from 1867 to 1868 and was active in the affairs of the Congregational church, where he served as the organist for more than forty years.

In 1860, Henry married Phoebe Loraine Andrews of New Salem. They had three children—Marion Andrews, Alfred Waldo and Edward. On August 30, 1883, Edward Payson married Charlotte Woods of Enfield, a cousin of Amanda Woods Ewing. Edward and Charlotte did not have children.

In 1902, Edward, a man "of genial temperament, kind-hearted, generous and beloved throughout the town,"[66] died of heart failure. A *Ware River News* story detailed how Henry generously remembered his brother by giving each employee a gift. For women it was five dollars in gold, and for men it was cloth for a suit. The gifts were "appreciated by every employee of the company and…entirely unexpected." Of Edward, the story noted that the workers "feel they have lost a dear friend and his many acts of kindness will be missed."[67]

Henry, "so shattered…that he never recovered his former vigor," died of heart disease just four years later. His obituary in a Springfield newspaper noted that "Mr. Smith was honest and upright in all his dealings and was long identified with the business interests of the town. He gave generously to all worthy causes, and his death is felt to be a personal loss for the community."[68]

After the losses of Edward and Henry, the business of the Swift River Company fell to Henry's sons, Alfred and Edward. By this time, the textile industry had begun to shift to larger, consolidated entities with more advanced technology, many of which had been built in the South after the Civil War. The third generation of Smith brothers surely felt the impact. After just six years of running the business, they placed an advertisement in the *Wall Street Journal* announcing the sale of the fully intact mill with enough stock to operate the plant for fifteen days.

The 1912 advertisement described Enfield as "a very pretty village," an "independent, well-to-do, high-class community, not spoiled by the many fads of the day." According to the ad, Enfield was prosperous, with "concrete sidewalk all the way" and three sources of electricity in the process of being installed. The ad also highlighted the value of the Swift River, "a river that not only furnishes all motive power the plant needs for nine months in an average year but it also supplies it with pure soft water."[69]

The Swift River Company sold on December 20, 1912, to a local man, David A. Jennison of neighboring West Brookfield, former proprietor of the Swift River Hotel. This change of hands made townspeople and especially Smith's employees worry for their livelihoods, as "it was feared by many that [the company] would be shut down." When it was announced in January that Jennison would organize and open the Grant S. Kelly Company on January 27, 1913, local papers reported that employees and Enfielders alike were "rejoicing" over the announcement that "present employees are requested not to leave town, as they will be wanted."[70] The Smiths remained landlords for a time, but in later years, they put the houses they owned up for sale, and many were purchased by their tenants.[71]

While Smith's Village had its own company store, railroad station and school, its residents had to travel the mile south to Enfield Center for church and other business. Enfield's Main Street was the most bustling of those in the valley towns because it had two churches and a chapel, a grange building, a town hall and schoolhouse, several general stores, a doctor's office, a hotel, a gas station and a pool hall—in addition to the railroad station, the Tebo Mill (formerly the Minot Manufacturing Company) and the firehouse.

Heading south into Enfield Center from Smith's Village, one would pass first by many residences, including the grand home that belonged to Marion's uncle Edward Payson, then by the town's civic and religious buildings: the Methodist church, the schoolhouse, the town hall and the Congregational chapel on the left side of Main Street and the Congregational Church with its nearby cemetery and the Soldier's Monument and town common on the right. Beyond these buildings and other houses lay the town's business district, at the intersection of Main Street with Bridge Street to the south and Hill Street to the north.

Just before Bridge Street stood a building owned by Howard D. Paine, known as Paine's Block or the Barlow Building. On the corner of its first floor was Dr. Segur's office. Doc would see patients there or at their homes, where he'd perform sick calls and sometimes even operations, by himself or with trained assistants such as visiting nurses.

If a patient needed to go to the hospital, Doc would accompany them to Springfield on the Soapstone Limited, where he kept a cot in the baggage car.[72] When they arrived, an ambulance would meet Doc and his patient and drive them to Springfield City Hospital, considered to be on the leading edge of the medical field at the time. Established in 1870, by 1887 it had fifty beds, and by 1896 it had installed a surgical pavilion.[73] In later years, Doc also took patients to Mary Lane Hospital in neighboring Ware, which was closer and smaller, though no less well regarded. Doc served as the first chief of staff at the Ware Visiting Nurse and Hospital Association (WVNHA), before it became the Mary Lane Hospital.

Down Bridge Street and across the railroad tracks was Doc Segur's house, with its magnificent flower gardens kept by Doc's mother, who lived with the family. The Howes also lived on Bridge Street right next to the Segurs. Like Doc, Edwin Howe could walk from his house to his general store on Main Street, just after Bridge Street.

The first business on that block was another general store owned by Charles D. Haskell; next came the Masonic block, with the Bethel Masonic Lodge; and finally, the southernmost section, where the Howes' post office and general store attracted just about everyone in town.

Around the beginning of the twentieth century, small-town general stores functioned as the center of a town's social scene, where much of its business was conducted, and people connected with each other and the outside world through the post office.[74] Edwin Howe served as postmaster from 1889 to 1914, and his son Ned later took over the role from 1927 until the end in 1939.

Underwood remembers Enfield's general store "chiefly by its permanent odor, in which there were suggestions of dried codfish, pickled mackerel, spices, snuff, plug tobacco, molasses, and new rum, reenforced in cold weather by the evaporation of tobacco juice upon a hot stove, and the occasional whiff of a pipe."[75] According to their advertisements, the Howes'

Howes' general store and post office. *Personal collection of Edwin Howe's great-grandson Peter Howe.*

store offered "fresh fruit every Monday and Thursday," "fresh bakery foods every morning" and "a tub of fresh Vermont butter every week."[76]

Near the Howes' store was a building owned by Charles Felton, who leased the first floor to A.H. Phillips, a grocer, and a meat market.

Enfield's Main Street and Bridge Street intersection also featured a gas station and auto mechanic at Donald Rowe's garage and a three-table pool hall owned by the Lisk brothers, one of whom was James "Jimmy" Lisk. James was known as the valley's "nature boy" for his collection of Native American artifacts and his expert hunting and trapping skills. He also worked as the Smiths' gardener and groundskeeper for many years.[77]

Across the street from the business block, also at the four corners, was the Swift River Hotel, operated by William Galvin. The twenty-eight-room hotel was decorated for the centennial with a portrait of George Washington, which matched a portrait of Abraham Lincoln hung on the town hall. It was the only hotel ever built in Enfield and one of very few such establishments in the Swift River Valley. Constructed in 1832 on the public stagecoach route to Boston, the hotel continued to serve as a convenient stopping place for an overnight stay or a hot meal with the coming of the railroad.

After emigrating from Ireland, Bridget "Delia" Tryon worked at the hotel in the 1910s. She was later recruited to the Smith home by Loraine and Marion, where she worked as cook and housekeeper for decades thereafter.

The hotel's dining room could seat hundreds, and the first floor included a large center hall, a parlor and an office. For Enfield citizens, the hotel served as a beacon of lively hospitality and warmth. As Howe states, "The lights from the largest business structure in town cast a cheery glow which added much to the cheerfulness of the near-deserted town in the winter months."[78]

According to Howe, during the centennial, more than three hundred people enjoyed a "very satisfactory feast" in the hotel's dining room.[79] Additional diners were served meals prepared by a caterer in a nearby tent.

Later that evening, after dinner, attendees headed down the street for another special event: the Old Home Day celebration in the town hall.

Chapter 4

OLD HOME DAY

Like the Congregational church and the rest of town, Enfield's two-story brick town hall was decorated inside and out for the occasion. The hall was crowded the evening of Monday, July 3, 1916, with Enfielders of all generations sitting side by side on its wooden benches for the Old Home Day celebration.

The evening's program was designed to celebrate the town's history and welcome home former residents. Those who could not attend sent telegrams, letters and poems to be read to the crowd. The readings were enlivened by musical selections and refreshments, and the evening concluded with dancing. But perhaps the most exciting part of the event involved technology. People could view stereopticon views of Enfield, three-dimensional images created by combining two slightly different images of the same view using a special slide projector. And they could also watch short moving pictures of Enfield, its people and places. The town hall was already outfitted for this because Donald Howe had purchased equipment to show films once a month at what he called the Enfield Gala Theater.

A slide included in the film requested cash contributions for the centennial, stating that the film's purpose was to document and thereby "perpetuate Enfield's Centennial Celebration for years to come, that the future generations may view with pride the achievements of their fathers and grandfathers."[80] This hopeful message made two assumptions: that the event would be a success worth looking back on and that there would be future generations to look back on it. While the former would prove true, the latter would not, in

Exterior of the town hall, decorated for the centennial. *Swift River Valley Historical Society.*

part because Enfield was unable to provide the economic opportunities and job prospects needed to keep its best and brightest at home.

The town had a rich history of sending its residents out into the world to find opportunity and success elsewhere. Underwood underscores Quabbin's limited economic prospects when he wrote that by 1893, farms yielded "little return" and "the owners must pick up a living as best they can; the thin and stony soil can do no more for them."[81] For Underwood at least, the valley's challenging way of living, at first a point of pride, became a point of weakness.

Though the valley towns grew in numbers and prospered economically through the first half of the nineteenth century, they began a slow population decline in the latter half of the 1800s. According to the state census records, between 1850 and 1890, the four towns together lost more than one-third of their population. By the 1916 centennial, the valley's population totaled just over two thousand residents and was steadily declining. Four years later, in 1920, all four valley towns would be included on a federal census list of the 29 Massachusetts towns (of 354 in the state) that were not gaining in population.[82]

This decline was no doubt related to simultaneous declines in manufacturing and agriculture, which meant that Enfield and the valley had few jobs to offer their own residents, never mind new ones to attract new residents. Underwood discusses the exodus of young people born and raised in Enfield who, because of limited local prospects, went out into the wider world to find success and prosperity. He likens Enfield to a forest "which has been parted with most of its lusty and growing trees and consisted largely of old and wind-shaken trunks, with a few branches and sparse foliage." He believed those residents who remained in Enfield were "either without ambition and courage, or those whom duty and affection retained at home to take care of the old."[83]

In another nature metaphor that describes the flow of Enfield's citizens outward and away, Richards likened Enfield's population to the Swift River, "not itself a mighty stream, yet gathering up into itself smaller streams as it moves along." In this way, he said, the small town with narrow prospects "flowed along the course of its century of existence, and faithful lives, and [sent] out into the larger streams of state and nation whatever of mental, moral and spiritual enrichment and vital force its sons and daughters have developed and been able to contribute."

Richards declared that people are the chief product of any community, and Ewing noted that "to the world and its cities our little town has given generously of its best." They both listed a number of Enfield sons of some renown. These included Robert Field, for whom the town was named; Timothy Gilbert, an outspoken abolitionist who, like his brother Lemuel Gilbert, was also a celebrated piano-maker; Sylvanus Lathrop, a skilled architect who at age twenty designed the Congregational church steeple and later moved to Pittsburgh to build locks and bridges on the Monongahela River; Elihu Lyman, Enfield's first state senator, and other state senators, including J.B. Woods, Rufus Woods and Daniel B. Gillett; and nine ministers, including Robert Woods, Charles Ewing and Richards himself.

Of course, Francis Henry Underwood was named as the town's gift to the literary world as the author of *Quabbin* and more than ten other volumes; he was also a prominent abolitionist and a founder and assistant editor of the *Atlantic Monthly*. Edward Clark Potter was a sculptor of great renown whose specialty was animals, particularly horses. Potter was responsible for the General Hooker statue outside Boston's statehouse and the lions outside the New York Public Library, among many others.

Although Richards spoke only of distinguished Enfield men in his sermon, Ewing made sure to say that Enfield's daughters were not unknown, observing that many found "their place in the world of work" as stenographers, nurses, secretaries, librarians and teachers. She also mentioned the

> *countless other* [women] *who have gone forth to found and bless new homes…mothers who have labored faithfully and earnestly, that their children might have the advantages of which they themselves were deprived. As the children and grandchildren come home again, shall they not rise up and call them blessed?*

Ewing affirmed that opportunities at home in Enfield were limited, which necessitated its young people venturing out into the world—while those who remained in Enfield were happy to welcome them home again.

Of this exodus, Underwood writes, "From Quabbin well-trodden roads lead everywhere." This, of course, is the reverse of "all roads lead to Rome," a saying meaning that Rome was the cultural and intellectual epicenter of the world and which was no doubt the inspiration for the Enfield centennial's slogan, "All roads lead to Enfield." For this one long weekend in July 1916, Enfield did become the center of the world for its current and former residents, as it welcomed its sons and daughters back for its milestone birthday.

While there were certainly men and women of accomplishment and even fame among Enfield's native sons and daughters, most Enfielders lived modestly. In oral histories, many valley residents describe their way of life as simple, with no more than basic needs being met. Prescott and most of Greenwich did not have paved roads, and both towns lacked electricity and telephone service.[84] Most valley residents earned their livings as farmers or mill workers, and many lived in poverty.

Many homes had a wood or coal stove in the kitchen for cooking and heating. People piped water into their homes from the streams and springs originating from the Swift River. In 1916, valley residents kept their perishables cold with iceboxes in their kitchens; ice was cut from the icehouse down by the Swift River, which would have been stocked with large blocks of ice from local lakes and ponds in the winter months, layered with sawdust to keep them cool throughout the summer. Furniture and clothing tended to be more utilitarian than ornamental.

While Doc Segur and the Howes were middle class, given their professions, Marion Smith and her brothers belonged to the upper class, with a family estate worth approximately $1 million. In *Before the Flood,* Rosenberg describes the complicated social structure of the valley, including the "grinding and oppressive" poverty of the millworkers who lived in Smith's Village, the middle class of manufacturing managers and the upper-class families like the Ewings and, of course, the Smiths, "who had a Rolls Royce and servants."[85]

According to Rosenberg, many residents' memories of the valley were that its people were essentially economic equals, a recollection that was not accurate. But however disparate the wealth of Enfielders in 1916, it is meaningful that rich and poor lived near each other and were not only aware of each other but attended school, church and social organizations together. Contrast this income diversity with today's growing economic segregation, in which people of different social classes are more likely to live in towns or neighborhoods with other people who make similar incomes. This disparity means that towns with more affluent residents provide significantly greater access to safety, higher property values and better schools and municipal services than do less affluent neighborhoods and towns. In Enfield, the middle- and upper-class residents who were more educated, like Doc Segur, the Howes and the Smiths, served as leaders and helped to make improvements in schools and other areas of the town, enhancing life for all residents even as they enjoyed a more affluent lifestyle themselves.

The Quabbin Club, a women's social club established in October 1897, offers a good example of this dynamic. The club was founded as part of the social movement of women's clubs that took place during the Progressive era, from the 1890s to the 1920s, with Marion as its founding president and Amanda Ewing as auditor. Like many women's clubs, it began as a social and literary club but eventually took on community welfare issues such as education, civic engagement and public health. According to its constitution, its objective was "the mutual improvement of its members in literature, art, science, and all the important questions of the day."[86]

The meetings took place in members' homes, and the club produced a booklet each year that outlined the overarching topic of study along with lists of members, dates of meetings, issues to be discussed, musical selections to be played, poems and books to be read and other news of the day. In the club's early years, annual topics of study centered around a country (e.g., Holland in 1897–98, America in 1901–2) and eventually included broader topics such as "Art and Miscellaneous Topics," "European Travel" and "The American Woman."

In the club's early days, members wrote long papers in advance of meetings, spending "hours, even weeks…in trips to the library in Springfield."[87] In fact, it wasn't until 1909 that refreshments were regularly served, because members spent so much time reading papers and studying the designated meeting topic.

According to Donald Howe, the Quabbin Club "was the mecca of thousands of club members throughout the state during its forty-one years of activity. Speakers of wide renown were heard at the Enfield gatherings, and the club also maintained a vigilant eye on the town's civic affairs." The club sponsored a small plot of land in the center of Enfield that they maintained, including a community Christmas tree that they lit during the holiday season. The club took an interest in other civic issues, from supporting the local Red Cross to purchasing Liberty bonds, and worked to improve life for all in the valley.

Other social organizations in Enfield included the Bethel Lodge of Masons, in existence since 1825 and reorganized in 1858, in which Edwin Howe was quite active, holding every officer position at various times;[88] the Zion Chapter of the Eastern Star, a Grange organized in 1904 with a membership of over one hundred residents; the Joseph Hooker Chapter of the Daughters of the American Revolution, to which Marion belonged; the Boy Scouts; a Mother's Club; the town's Grand Army of the Republic post; and a volunteer Fireman's Association led for many years by Doc Segur, which, when not fighting fires, devoted much of its free time to planning social affairs, including the town's annual firemen's ball.

Doc's leadership of the fire brigade was well regarded, as evidenced by a letter sent to him in September 1915. Doc had been sick for some time, unable to go to work. His colleagues wrote to say that at their last meeting, the department voted unanimously "to extend you a letter expressing our sincere sympathy for you in your present illness. You have the good wishes of every member of the Department for a speedy recovery; further evidence of our wishes will follow later." In his return letter, Segur called the gifts, whatever they were, "both elegant and useful"; however, "far more than that," he wrote, "I prize the spirit of sympathy and friendship that it brings to me from them."[89]

This spirit of friendship and fellowship, deeply enmeshed in the social fabric of Enfield and the valley, was celebrated at the old home day gathering that evening as current and former residents gathered in the town hall to celebrate one hundred years of community. As they made their way home that evening, they looked forward to the third and final day of centennial events on the nation's birthday, July 4, 1916.

Chapter 5

A Parade to Remember

Tuesday, July 4, the final day of the centennial, dawned brighter, with cooler temperatures following Monday's rain, though a fine rain descended in the afternoon.[90] Enfielders and many out-of-towners filled Main Street early that morning, eager to enjoy the grand Fourth of July parade, which "made a spectacle such as western Hampshire has scarcely ever before seen equaled."[91] The *Athol Transcript* reported that more than eight thousand people turned out to watch the parade that day and that "no town in the section has ever surpassed [Enfield's centennial parade] in general beauty, interest and elaborateness." The newspaper declared, "It will give Enfield something to talk about for years to come."[92]

The parade began on Ware Road at nine thirty in the morning and proceeded to Smith's Village, then returned to the judge's stand on the town common via Main Street. Clinton Powell served as chief marshal, and with him in the lead were policemen on horseback, including Enfield chief of police Harry Hess, followed by the Greenfield Military Band. Then came dozens of floats with flags, greenery and other embellishments decorating horses and carriages, automobiles and people on horseback and on foot.

The parade also featured the volunteer fire department, which walked with their engine, and an assortment of "horribles." This tradition dated back to the 1850s and had its origins in Lowell, where the working class first parodied the oldest chartered military organization in the United States, the Ancient and Honorable Artillery, by dressing in shabby, ill-fitting clothes and performing what they called the Antiques and Horribles Parade. This

Horses and carriages decorated for the centennial parade. *Swift River Valley Historical Society.*

spoof was replicated in many Massachusetts towns in subsequent years, and Enfield's horribles featured clowns and other oddly dressed jesters.[93]

Then came the floats. Entries from individuals and organizations competed for prizes in various categories, including best decorated carriages and automobiles. First prize for best antique float went to Walter Bliss for his log cabin, which was a real cabin made of bark slabs, complete with interior decorations. Second place went to Smith's Village industry for their "water wheel of flowers" float.

The Belchertown Grange took the fifteen-dollar prize for best decorated float, on which three women represented the three Graces along with the goddess of peace with her emblem, the dove. The Greenwich Grange won fifteen dollars for best decorated automobile, covered in greenery and dotted with yellow roses. The Quabbin Club and Daughters of the American

Revolution's joint entry won the ten-dollar second prize for best decorated automobile, which featured the goddess of liberty with people of various nations at her feet, along with soldiers and a Puritan couple.

Following the parade, more sporting events and more speeches came the Fourth of July celebration everyone had been waiting for: the fireworks. As dusk fell over the valley, the centennial's events nearly at a close, residents may have pondered another kind of darkness that had appeared on the edge of the valley's consciousness two decades earlier in 1895: Boston's interest in the Swift River Valley as the potential location of a massive reservoir of drinking water, the final stop on Boston's westward progression of reservoirs of increasing size and capacity.

Richards had mentioned this possibility in his historical sermon two days earlier. Although he devoted most of his talk to describing Enfield's many gifts, treasures and values, Richards pointed out that in the past century, the state's population had grown from 50,000 to 8 million, and Boston had ballooned from 43,000 to 700,000 people, a sixteenfold increase. He then observed that the Swift River, which had fueled Enfield's growth in previous centuries, was likely to be the cause of its demise.

Richards spoke to his audience about the possibility of a reservoir in the valley in very real terms, outlining the Boston Water Commission's plans "to make the Swift River valley a great storage reservoir for supplying water for the cities in the eastern part of the state." He began to prophesy, saying that as he reviewed the commission's plans, he could imagine himself "standing some day on the top of Mt. Ram or Quabbin, and, looking down into the depths of a great lake, saying to some companion…'There I was born.'"

We cannot know how surprised Richards's listeners were at these predictions about the valley being flooded or how many of them took this prophecy at all seriously, but Reverend Richards's vision of a coming reservoir was certainly prescient. Within twenty-five years, the valley would be empty of people, stripped of its houses and landscape and slowly filling with billions of gallons of Swift River water to be piped away from the valley—all because Boston needed water.

PART II

WATER FOR BOSTON

HYMN BY GEORGE RUSSELL, ESQ.

*To be sung by the Handel and Haydn Society
and the Audience—Tune, "Old Hundred"
From Water Celebration Exercises at the Fountain on October 25, 1848*

Eternal! uncreated God!
Source of our being! Fount of love!
Our songs ascend to thine abode;
Thou art the joy of worlds above.

The Sea is thine:—at thee command,
From darkness deep, its waters came:
The "Sons of God" beheld they hand,
And in loud chorus praised thy Name.

Rivers, and lakes, and springs declare,
That Thou art wise, and kind, and good;
Both man and beast thy boundaries share:
Thou givest drink:—Thou givest food.

Behold! from yonder distant lake,
A stream, our city now supplies!
We bid it welcome:—come partake:
To-day its waters greet our eyes!

Let old and young, and rich and poor,
Join in one full harmonious song!
Let every tongue its praises pour,
And swell the Anthem loud and long!

Chapter 6

A City on a Hill

From the earliest times one of the most perplexing questions facing the city has been that of securing an adequate supply of wholesome water.
—Boston: One Hundred Years a City

When the Puritans landed in Massachusetts aboard the *Arbella* in 1630, they initially settled in present-day Charlestown. Because that area did not have an adequate supply of fresh water, they soon relocated a few miles south and across the Charles River on the Shawmut Peninsula, which had freshwater springs. In fact, the name Shawmut derives from the Algonquin word *mashauwomuk*, which is said to mean "living fountains" or "place of clear waters."

Built on an eight-hundred-acre peninsula connected to the mainland by a narrow passage that was partially submerged during high tide, Boston was practically an island—surrounded by water or tidal flats depending on the tides. Although the settlement would go on to flourish as a seaport, its location presented freshwater supply problems almost from the start. The Puritans' first small settlement there consisted of fewer than thirty houses. Residents piped water from springs into their homes. But nearly fifty years later, by 1673, the town had grown significantly, with more than 1,500 houses and sixteen to eighteen thousand people, and the peninsula's surface water was not adequate.[94] Residents then dug wells and collected rainwater in cisterns. The quality of this water was very poor; it was "hard, highly colored, often odorous, saline, bad-tasting, and sometimes polluted."[95]

In addition to its poor quality, there was not enough water available for fighting fires. More than fifteen major fires destroyed various parts of Boston in the eighteenth century; one in 1760 destroyed hundreds of buildings, and the Great Fire of 1872 consumed sixty-five acres and resulted in thirty deaths. These avoidable tragedies also highlighted the need for a larger water supply and better infrastructure to fight fires.

As American cities like Boston continued to grow significantly throughout the eighteenth and nineteenth centuries, local governments played increasingly powerful roles in their development, including creating water infrastructure. Although we take it for granted today, three centuries ago, Boston and many other cities debated whether water was a resource everyone was entitled to or a commodity people had to pay for.

Ultimately, Boston's decision was informed by its founding values. In his famous lay sermon written aboard the *Arbella* in 1630, John Winthrop, Boston's first governor, referred to the Puritans' new settlement as "a city

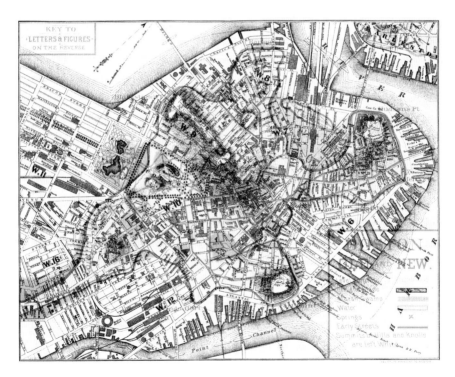

Map by historian Justin Winsor, superimposing original Shawmut Peninsula onto 1880 map of Boston. The interior line shows the peninsula's original shoreline. This image was a frontispiece for volume 1 of Winsor's *Memorial History of Boston, Including Suffolk County, Massachusetts*, 1882. *Digital Commonwealth Massachusetts Collection Online.*

upon a hill," with the eyes of the world upon it. Winthrop advocated strongly for Puritan values of charity, love of God and one another and, especially, for collective responsibility, as "care of the public must oversway all private respects." These ideals would continue to define the city's identity and influence its decisions in the centuries to come—including the solution to its water problems.[96]

The city's first large-scale water project was a private venture. In 1795, a company called the Boston Aqueduct Corporation installed a water system connecting Jamaica Pond to Boston via an underground network of wooden pipes. The system worked with gravity, so it could not bring water to residences at a higher elevation—and it provided water only to residents willing to pay for it. The system served just 1,500 of Boston's 20,000 homes, and it was not long before Jamaica Pond's waters became polluted.

Boston's attempts to solve its water problems began in earnest in the 1820s, when the population had reached forty thousand and counting. Boston was incorporated as a city in 1822. Beginning around that time, the municipal government took on infrastructure issues like disposing of sewage, filling in the tidal flats surrounding the peninsula (which doubled the city's landmass and led to the development of Back Bay[97]) and solving the city's growing need for fresh water. However, during the next two decades— despite earnest mayoral promises, the convening of many committee meetings, the conducting of studies and submission of reports by various experts, petitions from physicians and angry public demands—the city made no actual progress toward addressing its increasingly urgent need to improve the quantity and quality of its water supply.

Meanwhile, by 1842, nearby New York City had solved similar problems with a new water system that brought much-needed fresh water to its citizens from Croton in the north via a forty-one-mile aqueduct. The chief engineer on the project was John B. Jervis. The Croton system, which included the aqueduct, a dam and a reservoir, was perhaps the first example of a large American city reaching outside of its urban limits to increase its water supply. This project required the displacement of approximately two hundred rural residents.[98]

In 1845, when Boston was ready to hire yet another expert to find a solution for its water issues, Jervis was the obvious choice. Given his unique expertise and fame, he was granted a great deal of independence in his work.[99] After months of reviewing previous reports and completing new surveys, Jervis recommended using Long Pond in Natick, at a capacity of two billion gallons, which would provide Boston's residents with eighteen million gallons of pure water daily. The estimated cost of the project at that time was $3 million.

The general court passed Boston's Water Act in March 1846. Work began immediately on the new system, which included an aqueduct from Long Pond to a receiving reservoir in Brookline, which would distribute water to Boston via a system of pipes and smaller distributing reservoirs. Long Pond was renamed Cochituate, after an Algonquin word meaning "swift river" or "rushing water," and the entire reservoir system came to be called by the same name.

Like New York's Croton system, Boston's Cochituate system took several years to complete. And like New York, when it was done, Boston celebrated its new water supply with a holiday. On October 25, 1848, Bostonians waited on the common as Cochituate water made its twelve-hour journey from Natick to the Frog Pond Fountain on Boston Common. The description of the celebration in the *Boston Globe* captures the relief and excitement of this milestone for Bostonians after so many decades of water famine:

> *The city was awakened by the simultaneous roar of 100 cannons and the ringing of every church bell in the town and beyond. There would be no commerce that day, nor work, nor learning. The bridges leading to the city were early on crowded with neighbors come to share the glorious joy. The streets of Boston soon became impassable, and the long procession of dignitaries had a hard time getting through.*
>
> *"Do you want the water?" Mayor Quincy shouted to the upwards of 100,000 people assembled on the common as dusk fell.*
>
> *"Yes!" they roared back and with a mighty pull on the lanyard, the sluice shot open and a geyser leaped 70 feet into the air…*
>
> *It was, all in all, a grand and glorious fight* [to get water], *and a wonderful party in the end.*[100]

But Boston's relief was short-lived. Just a decade later, with the city's population approaching two hundred thousand, water usage rose to seventeen million gallons per day, beginning to exceed what Cochituate could comfortably provide. This increased usage was due not just to population growth; the introduction of indoor plumbing significantly increased water usage beyond what the Cochituate Water Board had foreseen in the 1840s.

As a result, the water board proposed that an additional reservoir be built and connected to the Cochituate system. In 1866, the city began construction on the 731-million-gallon-capacity Chestnut Hill Reservoir, which was built on 212 acres of land purchased from local residents. Seven additional storage

Illustration of water celebration exercises at Frog Pond fountain, October 25, 1848. *Digital Commonwealth Massachusetts Collection Online.*

reservoirs were constructed in the Upper Sudbury watershed between 1875 and 1898, providing an additional 10 million gallons of capacity.[101] The Sudbury River and Mystic Lake were also connected to Boston's aqueducts to expand emergency supply during drought conditions. The complete Cochituate and Sudbury systems, with all these additions, provided Boston with 62 million gallons of pure water each day.

As Fern Nesson wrote in her book *Great Waters*, the most notable outcome of the Cochituate system was a clear delegation of expertise and authority on water supply matters to the new three-member, professionally trained Cochituate Water Board. While for decades, the city's leadership and populace had debated all aspects of water—from public health issues to public versus private ownership—now the board would determine the city's future actions.

While the board had greater expertise, it also had its own proclivities. Nesson notes that early engineers were inclined toward "knowledge handed down by revered predecessors" versus new and emerging technologies; because the gold standard at the time was storage reservoirs that piped pure, gravity-fed water to municipalities, Boston's future actions were skewed by the board toward the construction of "large, future-oriented supplies."[102] This inclination would prove consequential as Boston's needs continued to grow and the city looked further west to quench its thirst.

Chapter 7

Boston Grows Thirstier

Let her stand fast by herself. She has grown great. She is filled with strangers, but she can only prosper by adhering to her faith. Let every child that is born of her and every child of her adoption see to it to keep the name of Boston as clean as the sun; and in distant ages her motto shall be the prayer of millions on all the hills that gird the town, "As with our Fathers, so God be with us."
—*Ralph Waldo Emerson,*
as quoted in Boston: One Hundred Years a City

By the late 1800s, Boston again saw water problems on the horizon as its water board predicted another shortage by 1898. In addition to continued population growth and increased indoor plumbing, a number of neighboring towns were appealing to Boston and the general court for help with their own water problems.

The city had recently addressed another infrastructure problem—sewage—through cooperative effort with surrounding towns. In 1889, the State Board of Health of Massachusetts completed a study that led to the creation of the Metropolitan Sewer District, a system of sewer drainage for Boston's entire metropolitan area. The study included a survey of all the drinking water sources in Massachusetts prepared by the board's chief engineer, Frederic Pike Stearns.

Like Jervis, Stearns was an experienced civil engineer. He was also considered to be a meticulous researcher, known for his fairness, good judgment and public spirit.

Stearns's thorough drinking water studies from the metropolitan sewage project made him the perfect candidate to spearhead the new study commissioned by the general court to "investigate, consider and report upon the question of a water supply for the City of Boston and its suburbs within a radius of ten miles from the State House."[103] In his completed report, published in 1895, Stearns recommended twenty-eight towns to be part of the metropolitan district,[104] projected population growth and water supply needs of the metropolitan district in future years and identified three possible sources of water for metropolitan Boston within a one-hundred-mile radius: Lake Winnipesaukee in New Hampshire; the Merrimack River, north of Boston; and the south branch of the Nashua River, west of Boston.

Given the complications of Winnipesaukee's location in a different state and the well-known pollution of the Merrimack River, Stearns ruled out the first two options. He then focused on the feasibility of creating a large reservoir near Clinton, Massachusetts, by impounding the Nashua River and piping that water to Boston through an aqueduct connected to the Cochituate system at Sudbury. Like the Cochituate system, the water would travel by force of gravity over the thirty-five miles east to Boston and would not require filtration.

This new reservoir at Clinton, which would hold more than sixty billion gallons, would double the metropolitan area's water supply. Perhaps what appealed to Stearns the most was that this plan—and further westward action—could permanently solve Boston's water problems. He wrote in his report:

> *The very great merit of the plan now submitted is to be found in the fact that this extension of the chain of the metropolitan water supplies to the valley of the Nashua will settle forever the future water policy of the district, for a comparatively inexpensive conduit can be constructed through to the valley of the Ware River and* beyond the Ware River lies the valley of the Swift [emphasis mine]*; and, in a future so far distant that we do not venture to give a date to it, are portions of the Westfield and Deerfield Rivers, capable, when united, of furnishing a supply of the best water for a municipality larger than any now found in the world.*[105]

Stearns envisioned a final solution for Boston's water problems, beginning with what would become the Wachusett[106] Reservoir near Clinton. Although he described the watershed area as "sparsely settled" and not suited to agriculture or manufacturing, there was a problem. People lived in Clinton and surrounding towns, and they would need to be removed before the new reservoir could be built. Stearns noted that the $19 million budget for the system could easily accommodate the compensatory payments required to purchase land from the 1,700 people living in the sections of Boylston, West Boylston, Clinton and Sterling in the watershed area and that population growth in the affected towns was slow and not expected to increase. In other words, the waters and lands of the Nashua watershed would be easy to take.

While Stearns's plan was well received in the engineering community, there were obvious objections from the people whose land would be taken. When the House and Senate Standing Committees on Metropolitan Affairs and Water Supply held open hearings on the bill in February 1895, the mill owners and residents of the towns of the Nashua River watershed expressed their disapproval. West Boylston's counsel Frank P. Goulding of Worcester spoke on behalf of the town:

> *We are in the position of the victim of this scheme….The only argument the victim has to present is a wail. I can prolong the wail, but after all it is only a plaintive cry that we have to offer as an argument…*
>
> *If you are bound to have our valley, the valley which our fathers founded, and every avenue of escape seems to be shut off, we want it to come and be done with. We don't want it referred to the next general court; that would be prolonging our misery. This suggestion has palsied all interests in West Boylston; we are living a living death, and we should deprecate, if the thing must come, any postponement or referring to the next general court.*[107]

Because Nashua watershed residents believed they had no hope of stopping the reservoir, they encouraged the general court to move forward quickly and decisively instead. West Boylston also requested amendments should the bill move forward: that the state should compensate business owners, property owners and workers whose livelihoods would be affected by its construction, even if they were not directly in the watershed area.

The Metropolitan Water Act was passed by the general court on June 5, 1895. The governor appointed the Metropolitan Water Board, which hired Stearns as its chief engineer. Frank Winsor, another experienced engineer, worked with Stearns to design and build the Wachusett Dam, which was constructed in 1897. Then a large aqueduct was built to connect the Wachusett Reservoir to the Sudbury and Cochituate systems. The aqueduct was purposefully built larger than necessary, should it ever be needed to convey water from the Ware and Swift rivers, as Stearns's report suggested it

Wachusett watershed from Pine Hill before the Wachusett Reservoir. *Digital Commonwealth Massachusetts Collection Online.*

Wachusett watershed from Pine Hill after the Wachusett Reservoir. *Digital Commonwealth Massachusetts Collection Online.*

might.[108] Construction of the Wachusett Reservoir was completed in 1905, and it was filled by May 1908.

At the time of its completion, Wachusett was the largest reservoir in the world, built to serve the towns of metropolitan Boston with a capacity of sixty-five billion gallons of water. The reservoir required the removal of 1,700 people from the twelve-square-mile watershed across portions of four towns acquired by the state, plus the demolition of six mills, four churches, eight schoolhouses, hundreds of homes, two cemeteries and nearly thirty miles of roads and railroads. Six and a half square miles of soil was stripped, and six million cubic yards of material was removed before the reservoir was filled with water.[109] West Boylston's Old Stone Church was the only structure left standing in the watershed, a reminder of the community's loss.

Residents of West Boylston, Boylston, Clinton and Sterling affected by the reservoir were paid for damages resulting from lost property and real estate. The state paid mill owners in the watershed area for their property and mill owners on the Nashua River for the loss of their waterpower. In addition, the state awarded annuities to the towns of Boylston and West Boylston to compensate for the loss of taxable property.

Though no towns were disincorporated to build the Wachusett Reservoir, four were diminished and changed, especially West Boylston. In 1903, the *Globe* reported that

> one visiting West Boylston today, acquainted with the town before the takings of the water board took place, would have much difficulty in getting his bearings. The little village is all torn up and what was once a lovely spot and the mecca of many summer visitors, is now a veritable desert.

However, the *Globe* noted, "a new town practically has sprung up about the Common, where many of the older residents, whose places were taken by the water board, have built new homes with the majority of money received for damages."[110]

The Wachusett system was expected to be adequate for at least fifty years. But by the time it was completed, drought years and new requests for water from other municipalities, such as Worcester, meant that Boston would need to look further west to expand its supply, this time toward Enfield and the Swift River Valley.

Chapter 8

THE GREATER GOOD:
CITY VERSUS COUNTRY

For the time being, Boston is unusually well supplied with plenty and wholesome water…but it is so difficult to stop waste that it has already been stated officially that unless means be found to prevent it, the time will not be far distant before new sources of supply will have to be secured at an enormous cost.
—Boston: One Hundred Years a City

B y the time of Wachusett's completion in 1905, Boston's leaders could foresee that the city would need more water in the not-too-distant future. They would soon face what New York City was already experiencing: rapid population growth (much of it due to immigration), increased water usage thanks to indoor plumbing and physical expansion of the city limits into five boroughs, all of which meant that the current water supply was no longer adequate.

In 1905, the same year Boston's Wachusett system was completed, New York State created the New York City Board of Water Supply, which purchased land in the Catskills to create a new reservoir system to carry water to the city via a ninety-two-mile aqueduct, then the longest in the world. One of New York's reservoirs, the Ashokan Reservoir, as it came to be known, required twelve villages and two thousand residents to be removed, more than ten thousand acres cleared, one thousand cubic yards of material excavated and nearly three thousand bodies exhumed from cemeteries.[111]

In the years that followed, the size and scope of this engineering project made news far and wide. A column in one of the Swift River Valley newspapers headlined "Villages, Farms and Cemeteries Go to Make Way for the Reservoir" detailed the engineering feats that required over two thousand souls "to make way for the march of progress."[112] A month later, the same paper ran an article about fifteen reservoir workers who died in an accidental explosion.[113] And in 1914, the *Springfield Union* highlighted the project's aqueduct as the longest tunnel in the world in their "Searchlight" column, which featured the "latest news from the fields of science, education, and invention."[114]

Frederic Stearns, chief engineer of Boston's Wachusett project, served as consulting engineer on New York's Ashokan project, and Frank Winsor also worked on the construction of its reservoirs and aqueduct. The project's chief engineer was J. Waldo Smith, head of the Aqueduct Commission of New York City, who then became chief engineer of New York's water supply board, directing the construction of the Catskills system.

New York City residents held a three-day celebration of their newly completed Ashokan Reservoir in the fall of 1917. By then, eastern Massachusetts had suffered unforeseen years of drought. In addition, both the metropolitan Boston population and water usage were growing even faster than anticipated, and more municipalities—such as Worcester, Waltham, Newton and Brookline—were struggling to meet their own water needs and expressed interest in joining the metropolitan Boston system.[115] Boston's water supply strained under this increasing pressure. Finally, in 1919, the state legislature tasked a joint board of the Metropolitan Water and Sewerage Board and the State Department of Health to investigate the present and future water supply needs of the commonwealth and identify possible water sources to meet those needs. Of course, Boston had considered this matter many times before, but the general court hoped that this new joint board might solve eastern Massachusetts's water problems once and for all.

Unsurprisingly, Frederic Stearns, the chief engineer for the Wachusett Reservoir, was asked to serve as consulting engineer on this new joint board, with his protégé X.H. Goodnough serving as secretary and engineer. Also on the joint board was Dr. Henry P. Walcott, chairman of the Metropolitan Water and Sewerage Board. But with Walcott's retirement in November 1919, followed closely by Stearns's death in December 1919, the board appointed new members: Dr. Eugene R. Kelley, commissioner of public health, as chairman and J. Waldo Smith, chief engineer of New York's

Ashokan project.[116] Walcott agreed to continue as adviser in his retirement, and several others served as consultants on matters such as geology, water filtration, waterpower and legal matters.

And so Goodnough stepped up to lead this new study of Boston's water supply. A Harvard graduate born in Brookline, Goodnough worked first as a railroad engineer, then for Boston's and the state's drainage commissions. Under Stearns, he worked on the Wachusett system and was consulting engineer for sewage disposal in New York Harbor. Goodnough also helped Providence, Rhode Island, develop its water supply system, working with Frank Winsor.

Goodnough came to be known as the earliest visionary and strongest proponent of a Swift River reservoir. He was familiar with the valley because of one of his favorite pastimes: fishing. The *Globe* would later write that

> *the fact is that no man has reason to know the waterways of Massachusetts better than this man Goodnough. He has fished every stream where trout respond to a fly. He has rowed or paddled to the sources of every Bay State river. He has traveled the State's water courses up and down and crisscross, often packing a canoe.*[117]

Goodnough's appreciation for the natural resources of the Swift River Valley would ultimately lead to the valley's submergence.

Led by Goodnough, the board worked for over a year to execute their charge to investigate the water supply needs of the people of Massachusetts, including the filtration of the existing water supply. Though they were due to submit their findings in 1921, they were granted a one-year extension. However, they tipped their hand in 1921, revealing that they would be recommending the further implementation of the plans first outlined in Stearns's 1895 report to expand Boston's water system west of the Wachusett to the Swift River Valley, which included the construction of a $60 million aqueduct and dam at Enfield that would eventually hold more than four hundred billion gallons of water for Boston.

When the Springfield papers reported news of the potential reservoir in late January 1921, they noted that an alternative to the Swift River might be available—to build water treatment plants throughout the state to filter the water supplies currently available. But, the *Republican* cautioned, "the commission believes this plan not to be feasible."[118]

Other potential water sources, such as the Merrimack or Charles Rivers, or even current sources, such as the increasingly contaminated Cochituate

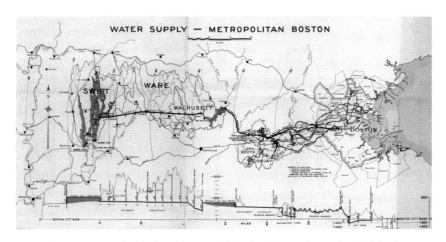

Map of Boston's reservoirs in Massachusetts. *University of Massachusetts Special Collections.*

Reservoir in Natick, would need to be filtered due to significant pollution from manufacturing. While it was possible to filter the water to enable drinkability, and it was potentially less expensive to install filtration than to build another reservoir, the board called disinfection "less reliable and more distasteful"[119] and said that the Swift River expansion would continue "the present high standards of quality to which the people of the district have become accustomed." Furthermore, the board stated, "it has long been the policy in Massachusetts to secure water supplies from unpolluted sources whenever they could be obtained, and to use natural protective measures to safeguard their quality."[120]

In 1922, when the board submitted its final report, it admitted that its charge was "so broad that it was necessary to place a limit on the extent of the studies made, corresponding to what could be accomplished"[121] and, further, that "it was natural for us to turn back to the report which the Massachusetts State Board of Health made to the Legislature in 1895."[122] Goodnough reported to the legislative committee on water supply that the extension of the Wachusett system was necessary in order to avoid water famine in the next decade.[123] He pointed to Boston's population growth, the metropolitan district's increased consumption and other towns' increasing needs, especially Worcester's, as reasons that steps should be taken immediately.

Most members of the committee saw two main advantages to Goodnough's plan over any other option: the Swift River water was pure and would not need to be filtered, and it could be fed to Boston via gravity and would not need to be pumped. This rationale, which echoed the reasoning for the construction of the Cochituate and Wachusett Reservoirs, had gained strength over the

Map of Quabbin Reservoir over existing Swift River Valley towns. *University of Massachusetts Special Collections.*

years and was practically unassailable at that point. After all, the Wachusett aqueduct had been built to accommodate the additional waters of the Ware and Swift Rivers in the future.

All members of the board were in favor of the final recommendations—but one. Chair of the Metropolitan District Commission James Bailey dissented, believing that estimates of the future population growth and the water supply needs of the metropolitan district were inaccurate and that Boston's water problem could be solved by filtering its current supply and building a small dam on the Ware River at a future date.

Bailey later expressed concern about the taking of lands that the project would require. Goodnough was recommending that four whole towns be disincorporated and flooded, which meant that more than two thousand residents would be required to leave their homes. While Wachusett and Ashokan certainly set precedents for this type of action, this new reservoir for Boston would be the largest and most disruptive to date, with 120,000 acres of land (187 square miles) taken for the massive reservoir's watershed. Yet Goodnough's description of the Swift River Valley sounded eerily like Stearns's of the Nashua watershed towns in 1895; Goodnough said the land consisted "mainly of abandoned farms, for which the state would have to pay little."[124] In other words, Goodnough expressed no concern about taking the rural towns for eastern Massachusetts's benefit, nor did he think it would be difficult to do so.

Like the residents of the Nashua River watershed and New York's Esopus basin before them, the people of the Swift River Valley were ready to fight for their homes—though they had little hope of winning, and they knew it. In the twenty-five years since the 1895 report first cast a dark shadow over their valley, they had seen both the Wachusett and Ashokan Reservoirs come to pass. And so, seemingly resigned to their fate, the Swift River Valley residents who spoke up echoed the plea of the people of West Boylston in 1898—that if Boston was to take their homes for the greater good, it would do so as quickly and compensate them as generously as possible.

Chapter 9

THE BEGINNING OF THE END

In 1922, the House and Senate Water Supply Committees held public hearings in eastern and western Massachusetts about the recommendations in the joint board's report. That spring, the people of the Swift River Valley found themselves fighting for their future in the Enfield town hall on an early May day, six years after their centennial.

The majority of the five hundred residents in attendance had one message they wanted to make clear: they opposed the Goodnough plan, but if their towns were to be taken to build a reservoir for Boston, it should be done as quickly as possible. Charles Felton, former member of the centennial's executive committee and current chair of Enfield's board of selectmen, proclaimed that valley residents "must not stand in the way of millions…but if you are going to take this valley, take it at once so that we may prepare to adjust ourselves to a new and different environment."[125]

The previous day, the engineers had been in Springfield and, earlier that same morning, in a similar brick town hall in Ware, where local manufacturers spoke about their dependence on the Ware River. Both these hearings focused on the economic impact that taking the Swift and Ware Rivers would have on mill owners and on the growth and prosperity of the region in general. According to the *Springfield Republican*, more than seventy people, from every affected town in western Massachusetts, attended the hearing in Springfield on May 4. Ben A. Hapgood of the Springfield Chamber of Commerce spoke of Springfield's rapid growth in the previous decade and said that "any diversion of [tributaries of the Connecticut

River's] waters would be detrimental"[126] to the Springfield area's further development. N.P. Avery of Holyoke agreed, saying, "The taking of these waters would undoubtedly result in checking the growth and expansion of this section [of the state]."[127]

The hearing in the Ware town hall the following day also focused on the "industrial handicap" that taking waters from the Ware and Swift Rivers would present for local businesses. Ware's state representative Roland Sawyer urged the general court to consider other sources, such as the Merrimack or Charles Rivers, and to show conclusively that filtration was not practical before proceeding with the Goodnough plan. Henry K. Hyde, president of the Ware Trust Company, "characterized the Ware River as the lifeblood of the valley and cautioned against the checking of its flow," while Judge Henry C. Davis said that by taking the waters of the Ware River, the metropolitan district would "eventually ruin every citizen in the community [of the Ware and Swift rivers]."[128]

Later that afternoon, the concerns at the Enfield town hall meeting were "more a question of sentiment"[129] than of industrial and economic interests. Swift River Valley residents "pleaded for immediate action," saying that homeowners were reluctant to spend money on repairs given the impending taking of their land. Some residents even claimed they might be willing to give up their land gracefully if the commission could convince them of the need for the reservoir. Those who protested cited water waste in Boston and dismay at exhuming their ancestors from cemeteries. They asked the general court to further explore filtration of other sources for Boston. Those residents who were willing to leave their homes implored the general court for a decision be made as soon as possible.

Despite these pleas for quick action, uncertainty continued to prevail. The general court held another hearing in Boston later that month, and twenty-five valley residents attended, requesting prompt action on the Goodnough plan. Though some speakers were "bitter against the bill," the *Globe* reported that the "balance were in favor, believing the interests of the State greater than those of the few who live in the four towns that will be destroyed."[130] Following this hearing, the water supply committees were asked to explore the possibility of filtering eastern Massachusetts water sources before bringing the matter to the next general court session. So the issue was pushed down the road into the following year.

At the general court's 1923 session, the Goodnough plan was reintroduced, and the water supply committees voted to undertake a yet another investigation into the water supply issue. Although the court authorized Governor Alvan

Fuller to appoint a disinterested engineer to head the investigation, he failed to do so because of a payroll dispute.[131] And so the committee turned to none other than Goodnough himself to review the Goodnough plan.

When the committee filed this new report in May 1924, after revisiting the Goodnough report with Goodnough's help, the majority of its members, unsurprisingly, endorsed the plan. But four members dissented, including Ware representative Roland Sawyer. Sawyer decried the lack of fair and adequate hearings for all who would be affected. He suspected not only that the claims about water shortages were exaggerated but also that Goodnough had falsely asserted this emergency to encourage the plan's adoption. For this reason, he expressed concern that no disinterested party had reviewed the plan and its claims.

The consensus of the dissenting members was that the general court should appoint a new commission to review all possible water supply options, including filtration of existing sources and the role of waste in current usage. The court agreed to appoint a Metropolitan Water Supply Investigating Commission to reexamine water needs and Goodnough's proposal. The commission was to hire a "disinterested engineer of acknowledged professional standing, qualified as an expert on water supply matters" to complete an investigation by the end of 1925.

Governor Fuller appointed three members to this new commission: chair Charles Gow, a Boston engineer; George Booth, publisher of the *Worcester Telegram*; and Springfield water supply engineer Elbert Lockridge. The *Globe* called the Gow commission the "compromise commission," given their mandate to consider "the moral right of Boston to go beyond the central divide of the State's water courses and seize upon a watershed that the cities and towns from Warren to Westfield look upon as the guardian of their ultimate destiny."[132] The Gow commission was under pressure to find a solution for Worcester's water needs as well.

The commission selected Allen Hazen as its consulting engineer. Hazen was a "well-educated and eminent professional" who had experience designing filtered water systems.[133] In 1897, he installed the first modern filtration plant on the Hudson River, which diminished Albany's typhoid cases significantly. He had also installed filtration systems for several large cities including Philadelphia, Pittsburgh and Providence.

Hazen's investigations led him to agree with Goodnough that water use would continue to grow and that conservation programs would not quell this demand. He praised the Wachusett system's abundant supply and low cost, saying that "perhaps no other single act has contributed as much to the health, happiness and prosperity of the residents" of the metropolitan district.[134] He agreed with Goodnough that the Cochituate and Sudbury systems were too polluted to be used and should be taken offline. He also believed that the plan to use Ware and Swift River waters would be ideal in terms of abundance of supply. However, he expressed concern that the cost to build a massive reservoir at Enfield would be too great.

Hazen offered a counterproposal: to build a smaller, less expensive reservoir at the Ware River in Barre, along with a compensatory reservoir to protect manufacturing interests along the Ware River. He also recommended that the waters of the Assabet River be comingled with Wachusett water to increase supply. This, along with filtration of the metropolitan district water supply, would meet the needs of Boston until approximately 1950, at which point he proposed that a reservoir be built at Topsfield using Ipswich River waters and that the Hobbs Brook Reservoir be raised to meet the city's needs thereafter.

Though the commission appreciated Hazen's efforts, which did indeed demonstrate viable alternatives to Goodnough's plan, they only halfheartedly recommended the new plan to the general court, noting they were not sure there was a better or simpler solution than Goodnough's if the district's projected water needs were accurate. And once the public learned of Hazen's plan, there was widespread opposition to it from residents across the state, because it would affect a number of communities along the Ware, Assabet and Ipswich Rivers. As Nesson notes, these towns had never been mentioned in any water supply solutions, "and they were by no means resigned to failure as an outcome" in the way the people of the Swift River Valley had become after so many years of uncertainty.[135]

The towns that would be affected by Hazen's proposed alternative organized and made their vigorous opposition known at several hearings. Eastern Massachusetts towns Framingham, Marlborough, Northborough, Lowell and others loudly proclaimed their objection to the state taking their lands and also to filtering their existing water systems. In the face of this resistance, the house and senate water committees removed the Ipswich and Assabet Rivers from the Hazen plan.

During this same period, Swift River Valley residents continued to make their opposition to Goodnough's plan known while simultaneously requesting to be put out of their collective misery should the plan go ahead. The *Globe* called the valley's opposition to the Gow and Goodnough plans "another phase of the old conflict between country and town....The country sees no reason why it should be sacrificed to serve the needs of swollen populations in the industrial centers." The *Globe*'s description of life in the valley under the shadow of the potential reservoir was akin to West Boylston's "living death," as described by counsel during the Wachusett hearing; the *Globe* reported that "nobody but a confirmed optimist invests money in improvements up Enfield way."[136]

In April 1926, Governor Fuller reviewed both the Goodnough and Hazen plans and requested that Gow, Goodnough and J. Waldo Smith work together to see if they could find a compromise between the two proposals. After deliberating for just one day, the three men returned to the water commission with their answer: the Goodnough plan should be adopted, because it would solve Boston's water problems completely and forever.

Although some wrangling in the statehouse ensued over how Worcester's water supply would fit into the plan, it was clear that Goodnough had prevailed. As the *Globe* triumphantly reported,

> *The only objection ever urged against* [the Goodnough plan] *was its cost....The community in which it was proposed to build the reservoir seems to be steadily losing inhabitants; there would be little trouble from that source. The water is of the highest grade and need not be filtered or purified in any other way, and would be delivered by gravity.*[137]

What's more, the Goodnough plan had the "endorsement of J. Waldo Smith, known throughout the world for his work as Chief Engineer of the New York Board of Water Supply in connection with the Catskill water supply of that city."

On May 18, 1926, the Goodnough bill was amended so Worcester would pay over $1 million for use of waters from the Quinepoxet River,[138] where it would build an additional storage reservoir. At an all-day hearing on May 20, the bill was debated at length and several additional amendments proposed, including one that would authorize the immediate taking of Swift River Valley lands in an effort to provide relief for residents who wished to sell at once rather than wait for the reservoir's construction to begin. This was in response to testimony from valley residents like J.H. Johnson of Dana, who said, "We have been in the 'valley of doubt' long enough. We want some decision."[139]

Although the Ware River Supply Act was passed by the senate and the house and then signed by Governor Fuller on May 29, 1926, the Swift River Act took nearly another year to complete. In February 1927, another hearing was held in Enfield's town hall, this one attended by both the joint board and the Metropolitan Water Supply Commission. By this time, valley residents knew the reservoir's construction was inevitable, so they continued to argue for fair treatment and immediate relief as they faced their fate. In an article titled "Doomed Towns Ask Swift End," the *Boston Globe* quoted the voices of many valley residents who urged haste. Again, J.H. Johnson said, "The people of this valley want justice and nothing more," while Doc Segur pleaded with the committee "to do unto these people as you would be done by."[140]

Three months later, the Swift River Act was signed on April 26, 1927. Together, the Ware and Swift River Acts authorized the construction of a tunnel at Coldbrook in Barre to divert Ware River water to the Wachusett Reservoir. Then the state would acquire the Swift River reservoir watershed lands, and the Wachusett-Coldbrook tunnel would be extended to the Swift River. Finally, two dams and a storage reservoir would be constructed at Enfield in accordance with Goodnough's 1922 proposal, which would impound 412 billion gallons of water in a thirty-eight-square-mile reservoir that would encompass the whole of the Swift River Valley. And with that, after thirty years of uncertainty, the valley's fate was sealed. Now all that was left was to make four towns—and every one of their residents—disappear.

PART III

DESTRUCTION

HOME, SWEET HOME

By an unnamed Swift River Valley resident,
from The Lost Valley *by Donald Howe*

They tell us they have paid for our land—
They tell us that our homes have been well sold—
But do not folks in Boston understand
There are some things you cannot buy for gold?

My humble home now seems more dear to me
Than any city mansion ever will;
No fairer outlook will I ever see
Than from my window out on old Den Hill.

Here as a careless, happy child I played,
And never thought or cared from here to stray;
There in the churchyard are our loved ones laid,
And here in peace had we still hoped to stay.

The roads and fields haunted with memories seem—
Fond memories of a bygone happy year.
We may not loiter o'er them now and dream
Of scenes and faces once to us so dear.

Our honored sires who helped this town to make,
Cut off the forests, cleared the fields from stones,
Their quiet graves they now must all forsake—
There is no rest here even for their bones!

We may not for our fields and forests mourn;
To leave our homes may be a passing gain.
To see our loved ones from the churchyard torn
Brings all our grief and sorrow back again.

Dear valley, soon must all your beauty fade,
And all your loveliness will pass away.
Stripped of your homes, stripped of your trees and shade.
And waters poured on ruin drab and gray.

The sun will shine as brightly as of yore,
And sparkling water will reflect the light,
But we will stand in grief upon the shore
And weep for scenes now hidden from our sight.

The busy mill, the little fertile farm
Whose produce seemed to fill our ev'ry need;
Those simple sports that had for us such charm,
When for a time from labor we were freed.

The young, perhaps, may leave without regret—
The ties that bind them are not yet so strong—
But we, the old, we never can forget
The homes which we have lived in and so long!

But backward still our thoughts will ever turn,
To lie in memory that happy past;
For our old friends and home our hearts will yearn
In grief and pain until the very last.

Those dear old friends now scattered far and wide,
The friends we loved, so constant and true,
No friendships like the old ones true and tried
Can ever be as dear to me and you.

Friends of our youth bound to us with a chain,
Whose links are made of loving deeds and kind.
Nor can we ever hope to forge again
With some new friends a tie so strong to bind.

Slow and reluctant we the valley leave,
With lingering look and eyes that fill with tears;
Our hearts will for the valley ever grieve
Through all our few and sad remaining years.

No other spot will seem so fair,
No other flowers will ever bloom so free,
No other home will with this home compare,
No matter where that other home may be.

And, city folks, do not our grieving scorn,
Nor view our homes with a disdainful eye.
Remember, it's the home where we were born,
And is the home where we had hoped to die.

EXILE.
Greenwich Village, April 5, 1932

Chapter 10

THE DECADE OF DESTRUCTION

Sadly whispered farewells were in order as Enfield walked down the valley of silence, down the dim, voiceless valley to its eternal doom.
—*Dora C. Foley in* The Lost Valley

With the Ware and Swift River Acts passed and the Commonwealth of Massachusetts poised to begin the construction of metropolitan Boston's new reservoir, the Swift River Valley residents felt "defiant, bewildered, saddened" as they braced for their long, slow march toward destruction.[141] The valley was already in a state of deterioration, given that people had known for thirty years that the reservoir was a possibility and for the last five that it was a probability. But now, with the reservoir a certainty, the valley's destruction became purposeful and all-consuming.

The state's first order of business was the Wachusett-Coldbrook aqueduct, a tunnel that would divert surplus water from the Ware River to the Wachusett Reservoir. In 1926, the commission began the process of purchasing nearly one thousand acres of land from twenty-six homeowners (affecting approximately one hundred residents) in the village of Coldbrook between Barre and Oakham. The commission was reportedly "well pleased" with the negotiations for this purchase, because the homeowners were compliant and the threat of eminent domain was not needed.[142]

Laborers then began the dangerous, claustrophobic work of digging the shafts of the subterranean aqueduct. On May 11, 1927, X.H. Goodnough,

Engineers at Rutland, captioned "Guests at the 'Blasting Party'" by the *Boston Globe*. *Left to right*: X.H. Goodnough, J. Waldo Smith, S.W. Horne, Frank E. Winsor, Davis B. Kenniston. *Swift River Historical Society*.

J. Waldo Smith, Frank Winsor and two other engineers were close by in Rutland, Massachusetts, when the first fifty-four sticks of dynamite were detonated with a blast that "sent state officials and world-famous engineers scuttling for cover."[143] That explosion marked the start of the Ware and Swift Rivers project, which would continue in earnest for more than a decade.

After completion of the aqueduct, a secondary diversion tunnel to bring Ware River water into the Quabbin was also constructed. The large, horseshoe-shaped tunnels, approximately twelve feet high and eleven feet wide, ran parallel to one another at a depth of between 250 and 650 feet. After digging to the appropriate depth, the workers would drill, blast and excavate the length of the tunnel, then line it with concrete.[144]

Construction of the Quabbin Reservoir itself did not begin until the 1930s, but a significant amount of preparatory work started in the late 1920s. Engineers arrived in the Swift River Valley in droves to begin the years-long process of marking property boundaries, photographing every structure and piece of property before its purchase and removal and preparing to move bodies from the valley's cemeteries.

The commission set up offices on Enfield's Main Street, above Harry Hess's meat market. It also purchased the former Chandler mansion—just a short distance from Bridge Street, where the Segurs and the Howes lived—as its headquarters. These central locations put the engineers right in the middle of Enfield, among the remaining residents, who did not welcome them—at least initially. These outsiders, mostly young, college-educated men from MIT, Northeastern and Worcester Polytechnic Institute, "antagonized [valley residents] almost from the first," according to Elizabeth Rosenberg, whose book *Before the Flood* focuses on the engineers and their relationship to the residents. The engineers were insensitive and "thoughtless in approach" to the people whose lives they were uprooting, perhaps not realizing that they were "living day-to-day reminders that the end was coming." Over time, however, the engineers adapted to life in the valley, and the valley people adapted to them, too. They became part of the social fabric of Enfield, forging relationships with its residents, leading social organizations and developing their own connections with the local landscape.[145]

If anyone still hoped that progress on the reservoir project might be halted, the events of the early 1930s convinced them otherwise. Perhaps the final nail in the valley's coffin was fixed in February 1931, when the Supreme Court ruled in Massachusetts's favor in a suit brought by the State of Connecticut, which sought an injunction to halt the construction of the Quabbin over

Tunnel construction circa 1933. *Metropolitan District Commission via Digital Commonwealth.*

riparian rights to the Swift River. Just a month later, in March, the first water from the Ware River was diverted through the newly completed aqueduct to the Wachusett Reservoir. In 1932, the commission broke ground on the new Quabbin Park Cemetery on Route 9 in Ware, the burial ground built specifically for reinterment of the bodies of valley residents. That same year, the reservoir project was officially named the Quabbin, which added a new layer of significance to the Nipmuc word for "the place of many waters."

In 1933, work began on the dike, the first of two barriers built to keep the waters of the Swift River in the valley; then, in 1936, construction began on the dam. The dam and dike were located in Enfield and were later named for engineers Frank Winsor and X.H. Goodnough.

The core walls of the dam and dike were constructed using caissons, rectangular watertight structures of concrete and steel that were forty-five feet long and nine feet wide. Laborers were lowered into the caisson chambers in large buckets, and they dug into the earth as the caissons sank down to bedrock under their own weight and sent the dirt they removed up to the surface in the same buckets. The caisson chambers were pressurized to keep water out, so the laborers worked forty-minute shifts and had to decompress (as divers do) when they emerged from the depths of the site. Once the caissons were at bedrock, they were filled with concrete and linked to other caissons, forming a watertight barrier at 125 feet below the level of the Swift River. Then the core walls of caissons were covered with hydraulic soil.

Laborers inside a caisson at the dam. *Department of Conservation and Recreation archives.*

The dike's main function was simply to contain water, while the dam was constructed with a diversion tunnel and a spillway to allow excess water to leave the reservoir. The *Globe*'s coverage of the construction throughout the decade was a bit breathless, expressing awe at the engineering marvels taking place at Enfield and even describing the blasted earth of the half-built dam in artistic terms: "beautiful in its way as many a highly appraised bit of natural loveliness."[146]

The dam and dike work sites swarmed with hundreds of engineers who, by 1937, were working night and day under lookout towers with searchlights and loudspeakers. The residents still living in the valley were keenly aware of the round-the-clock work, thanks to the light and noise at the construction sites, especially because from their locations in the south valley, the noise traveled northward through Enfield and the valley towns. Doc Segur's son, Bill, recalled standing on the porch with his father on a quiet summer evening when the stillness was broken by the rumble of steam shovels excavating the earth at the dike. He remembered the bitterness in his father's voice when he said, "Bill, they're digging our home right out from under us."[147]

In 1935, valley residents experienced another milestone loss when the Soapstone Limited, the railroad that had connected the valley's manufacturing to the outside world for sixty years, made its final excursions. The first trip was a widely advertised passenger run on May 26, 1935. According to the *Globe*, more than two hundred people from all over the state boarded the train at Springfield station. As the locomotive approached Enfield from the south, the first unmistakable signs of the reservoir were visible at the Winsor dam site, where construction materials were piled high and a crowd of engineers waved to the excursionists. Nearby, "a bare handful"[148] of remaining Enfield residents greeted the train. Passengers scrambled to capture photographs of what was left of the valley from the train's windows.[149]

A few days later, on June 1, the train made its truly final freight and passenger excursion. Howe noted that

> *every valleyite who could find the time was a passenger on that train, and those who were unable to make the trip either met the train at their home stations or at least gave it a wave as it passed by. One elderly woman who greeted the 'Soapstone Limited' from her window, had performed the same feat since the line was inaugurated sixty-three years before.*[150]

Earl, Delia and Marian Tryon were among those on board. If Marion, Doc or the Howes were not, they undoubtedly heard the familiar sound of the

"Taking up rails" at Enfield. *Metropolitan District Commission via Swift River Valley Historical Society.*

train pass by with a pang of sadness, knowing it was the last time they ever would.

The state purchased the railroad later that year. By 1936, the tracks and stations were gone, the railroad's route a ghostly path through the emptying valley.

Beginning in 1936, baffle dams were also being built at Greenwich Village where the Ware River entered the Quabbin to change the incoming flow, so the river water would fully integrate with the Quabbin's water before flowing back toward Boston. In addition, because the new reservoir would create an eighteen-mile-long impasse down the center of central Massachusetts, roads had to be diverted, and thirty-nine new miles of state highway were built around the valley.

For people living in the area during this decade, the reservoir's progress was inescapable and undeniable. Many had no desire to witness the devastation, and so the exodus began. In Prescott, so many residents left so quickly that the town turned its management over to the commonwealth in 1928. As early as 1929, 1,210 landowners in the watershed area had offered to sell fifty thousand acres to the state, and by 1934, the state had bought sixty thousand valley acres.[151]

In Enfield, Greenwich and Dana, some homeowners sold their land immediately but remained in the valley and rented their property back from the state. Others left altogether to avoid the inconvenience and the sadness of living in the doomed valley. Many of the residents who left early were young, but some were longtime valley people as well. Marion's friend Amanda Ewing moved to Springfield in 1928, though she did not sell her Enfield house immediately. Former board of selectmen chair Charles Felton sold to the state in 1928 and moved to Orange. As the wife of renowned sculptor and Enfield resident Edward Potter said of her family's decision to move, "I'm not bitter. The smaller must yield to the larger. Boston must have its water; and we must go. But, oh, I do not want to see the devastation!"[152]

The *Republican* made an accurate observation about the valley people at the start of the project:

> *Compelled though they are by necessity to accept the inevitable, they do not make any pretense of happiness in the disaster which has befallen them; they will go from their ancestral homes with dignity and composure when the blow finally falls; they will take up life again in other places and in new ways. But they will not pretend that this exodus is of their own choice or willing. And all the days of their lives they will mourn the tranquil beauty of those hills, those rolling plains, those sparkling streams, those ancient colonial houses, those drooping elms.*[153]

Chapter 11

LIFE AND DEATH IN THE VALLEY

Other valley people stayed until the bitter end, Marion Smith, Doc Segur and Edwin Howe among them. What they experienced in those eleven years is hard to fathom. They watched as each and every landmark and institution of the valley—many of which they'd either built themselves or contributed to—was dismantled and destroyed. They witnessed the beautiful landscape of their beloved valley altered past recognition, as every tree and all vegetation was eventually cut down. They were subjected to the constant noise of saws and axes chopping down trees and houses, of dynamite exploding and machinery clanking and roaring as the dam and dike were erected. They smelled the smoke of their neighbors' homes burning to the ground. They had to deal with their loved ones buried in the valley's cemeteries, some for generations—not only deciding where they should be reburied but, in some cases, needing to witness their remains being reinterred. So the decision to stay was not an easy one.

Marion, Doc and Edwin performed small acts of defiance in those eleven years. First and foremost, Marion and Edwin stayed in their homes and refused to sell to the state; they knew that, eventually, their properties and homes would be taken by eminent domain. Doc stayed as well, though he settled with the state just before Enfield was disincorporated in 1938. Marion, Doc and Edwin also did not make plans to leave Enfield until the town no longer existed. They refused to use the state-sponsored Quabbin Park Cemetery to reinter their lost family members. But by the time they left the valley in 1938, those difficult years had taken a terrible toll.

For a time, while the valley was being physically destroyed around them, its remaining residents managed to conduct a normal social life. During the late 1920s and early 1930s, Marion Smith continued to serve as a trustee of the Congregational church and president of the library association. She presented state reading certificates to elementary school students each year in the Congregational church chapel. Marion was also elected secretary and treasurer of the Cemetery Hill Company, hosting the group's early 1930s meetings at Bonnieview. She also furthered her interest in medicine, becoming chairman of Enfield's chapter of the Red Cross in 1932 and a director and life member of the Mary Lane Hospital Association in Ware in 1936. She and Doc were among the special guests at the Ware Rotary Club's Doctors', Dentists' and Hospital Day in Ware in 1933.[154] She hosted friends and family for stays at Bonnieview as well.

Other welcome developments held Marion's interest at home. In 1928, her cook and housekeeper, Bridget "Delia" Lahey, married the groundskeeper Porter Tryon's son Earl. The Smiths then hired Earl as a groundskeeper and chauffeur, so he, too, moved into Bonnieview with Delia. Two years later, Delia gave birth to a baby girl, delivered by Doc Segur at Mary Lane Hospital. Earl and Delia named the baby Marian Agnes for the two Marions in their life—Marion Andrews Smith, whom Marion Agnes would call Nana, and Earl's younger sister, Marion Blanche Tryon.

Marion Smith naturally took a great interest in her namesake, living under her roof. She showered Marian Agnes—nicknamed Tuda—with gifts from the moment of her birth.[155] According to Delia's careful notes about Marian's first years, Tuda's first steps with help were taken in Bonnieview's great hall on June 18, 1931. And for her first birthday, in September 1931, she had a cake with pink trimmings and a candle, along with a birthday ride in Nana's Rolls Royce. As she grew, Marion gave the young Marian other gifts as well, from piano lessons on her prized Steinway to professional photos taken on Bonnieview's grand staircase.

During this time, one more Tryon relation moved into Bonnieview. Marion hired Catherine "Kay" Sullivan, Delia's cousin, as a maid to assist Delia with household tasks and childcare.

These celebratory moments with the Tryon family stood in contrast to the immense losses Marion suffered during those same years. In 1928, Marion's mother, Loraine, fell ill with bronchitis. She died that August at the age of ninety. Delia devotedly nursed her in her final weeks, going above and beyond her duties as cook and housekeeper. To show their gratitude "in memory of our mother, and in appreciation of your faithful and loving care

for her during her long illness,"[156] Marion and her brothers gave Delia a $1,000 bonus, a sum that likely came close to her annual salary.[157]

Loraine Smith had lived in Enfield for seventy years and in the valley area for her whole life. She and Marion seemed inseparable, living together for Marion's entire life, traveling together and serving on town organizations together. There were rumors that Loraine made Marion promise never to marry, to stay with her always and keep the Smiths' money within the family.[158] Whether or not that rumor was true, the loss of her mother coupled with the impending loss of her homeland must have been a heavy burden for Marion to bear. Loraine's obituary notes that she died at Bonnieview and was survived by her three children, all of whom were living at home. She was buried at Cemetery Hill Cemetery behind the Congregational church.

Just seven months later, Marion suffered another blow when her brother Alfred Waldo passed away at the age of sixty-five from stomach cancer. Alfred was appointed postmaster of Smith's Village in 1892 and held that post for twenty-two years. Like his mother, he was buried at Cemetery Hill.

This left Marion and her youngest brother, Edward, to face a different type of loss: the destruction of the mill that was once the Swift River Manufacturing Company, the business that brought so much prosperity both to their family and to the town of Enfield. Though the Smiths sold the mill in 1912, it remained a landmark in Smith's Village, one inseparable from the Smith family's legacy.

The mill's "passing into history" was memorialized by the *Springfield Republican* in a lengthy article that paid tribute to its influence on Enfield's history. The buildings were emptied of their contents in 1929, the machinery sold to a Springfield junk dealer. The next year a Gardner, Massachusetts–based construction company purchased the mill buildings from the water commission and began to tear it down.[159]

The heartbreaks continued. On November 4, 1930, Marion's lifelong friend Amanda Woods Ewing died at age eighty. She had moved to Springfield two years earlier with her daughter and son-in-law but kept the house in Enfield and planned to return each summer.

Opposite: Marion Smith with baby Marian Agnes Tryon at Bonnieview. *Tryon family collection.*

Right: "Tuda" on Bonnieview's grand staircase. *Tryon family collection.*

Below: Earl and Marian Tryon with Marion Smith's Rolls Royce outside Bonnieview. *Tryon family collection.*

Perhaps the incessant losses proved too much for Edward Smith to take, because in March 1932, at the age of fifty-eight, he died of heart failure. Edward had served as president and treasurer of the Swift River Manufacturing Company from 1906 to 1912. Like his mother and brother, Edward was buried in Cemetery Hill. And now, at age seventy, Marion found herself alone, the sole heir to the Smith family fortune.

Chapter 12

GRAVE DECISIONS

After each family member's death, in 1928, 1929 and 1932, Marion chose to have them buried in Enfield, as though the reservoir were not being built and she would not have to move their bodies out of the valley in the near future. These decisions may have been small acts of defiance, or else Marion was in denial, because with every passing year, the reservoir's construction was becoming more obvious and consuming for the people of Enfield.

Between 1927 and 1933, when the new Quabbin Park Cemetery was completed, some six hundred bodies had been moved from valley cemeteries and reinterred elsewhere in preparation for the reservoir.[160] Marion was well aware of this as an officer of the Cemetery Hill Company, which met on October 8, 1928, to discuss the metropolitan commission's request to enter their cemetery to begin removing bodies. The company voted to grant permission.[161]

The commission chose Henry Clifton Moore, Enfield's professional undertaker (and the son of Edwin Moore, who helped dedicate the soldier's monument at the centennial) to lead the exhumation and reinterment of bodies in valley cemeteries. Moore was also the caretaker of many plots at Cemetery Hill. A few years later, in 1932, Moore sent Marion a letter to say he would "probably have to help the water commission quite a little on removals this summer and might not be able to attend to the [cemetery] lots at just the proper time," so he recommended that Roy Gage take over that responsibility.

In August 1932, a few months after Edward's death and burial, the commission requested that no further interments be made in valley cemeteries.[162] At that point, Marion must have known she had to choose a cemetery for her family's remains. But she did not face the matter until she was forced to, three years later. N. Leroy Hammond, division engineer of the Quabbin project, wrote to Marion, as he did to all family members of people buried in valley cemeteries, to confirm her relation to the deceased and request that she make plans for their reinterment outside the valley. Hammond wrote, "As you probably know, Cemetery Hill Cemetery is affected by the construction of Quabbin Reservoir and it will become necessary to remove remains now interred in this cemetery."

Within a week, Marion replied with a handwritten note—not the usual letter through her Ware attorney John Schoonmaker, as with her other Quabbin correspondence. The letter was scrawled on a small sheet of notepaper, front and back, apparently written in haste, as it included a number of sentence fragments and small errors. Marion confirmed her relationship to the deceased Hammond mentioned—her grandparents, parents and brothers—and said that she was their last living relative. She also added to the list her uncle, Edward, and his first wife, Charlotte, and requested that she might remove their remains as well, "as my father and uncle were never separated and were all the children in my grandfather's family."[163]

Marion concluded with uncharacteristic candor: "I hope this fall to make a decision regarding the place of removal of my dearest relatives and for my own interment. It is a very sad and painful duty—being obliged to make a change of resting place."

Within a year, Marion made her decision. Rather than choosing to move her relatives to Quabbin Park, which would have cost her nothing, Marion spent a substantial sum—$3,020, the equivalent of nearly $60,000 today—to purchase a family plot at the historic Springfield Cemetery in that nearby city.

The 1936–37 holiday season was surely a difficult one for Marion. Over the course of about a month, she had to spend several days at Springfield Cemetery to receive the remains of her nine relatives. The commission paid for the remains to be transported by hearse, and Marion was required to be present at the cemetery at the time of each relative's burial; if she did not appear, "the hearse would turn around, drive back to Quabbin Park Cemetery, and re-inter the body there."[164] Marion purchased new stones for the Smiths' grave site at Springfield Cemetery, including a tall granite monument with a draped urn atop it. When she made the plot layout, she saved a place for herself between her brothers.

Of the more than 7,500 bodies exhumed from the ten principal cemeteries and other private burial grounds in the valley, around 1,000 were not reinterred in Quabbin Park. Many valley people who selected other locations were motivated by ill will toward the commonwealth, wanting nothing to do with the state-sponsored burial ground. Some of Marion's friends made such decisions. Doc did not have any family buried in valley cemeteries, but he and Laura ultimately chose to be buried in Ware's Aspen Grove Cemetery rather than Quabbin Park, because—according to his son, Bill—he was "so bitter."[165] The Howes selected Belchertown's Mount Hope Cemetery for their immediate family, though many of their extended family members were reinterred in Quabbin Park and some at Forestdale Cemetery in Holyoke. Amanda Ewing chose Granby Cemetery because of her family's ties to that town. Others could not afford the luxury of an alternative cemetery, no matter how bitter they were.

No matter which cemetery people chose to rebury their loved ones, they shared significant concerns about the logistics of the exhumations and removals. As Rosenberg notes, many residents felt more upset about digging up their loved ones than about their own forced removal from the valley. Aware of this, the commission did its best to carefully catalog and photograph existing graves before removal. A *Springfield Republican* article that reads like a public relations piece for the new cemetery notes that the commission "surveyed all the cemeteries with meticulous care. It could destroy them all and set them up again, headstones and all, if there were any need of it. Every headstone has been photographed, every inscription has been recorded, every burial lot has been surveyed and recorded."[166]

Henry Clifton Moore and his team of laborers would carefully dig at grave sites until the coffin or body was reached. According to the *Republican*, most wooden coffins disintegrated in about ten years, and bodies often decomposed before the coffin did, so in many cases, there was little left to remove. But the workers exhumed whatever was left of the body—often just the skeleton—and any articles found with it. They placed the remains in a new wooden box, to be transported by hearse to the chosen cemetery and reburied there.

Many fear-based rumors circulated inside and outside of the valley, including concerns about the unmarked graves of white settlers and Native American burial grounds that would be inadvertently left beneath the Quabbin's waters. People heard gruesome stories about the dangers of contact with decomposing bodies, including false accounts of exorbitant salaries, required vaccinations and mandated quarantine for cemetery

Commission worker outside Enfield's Congregational Church Cemetery tomb. *Metropolitan District Commission via Digital Commonwealth.*

workers. No doubt the most repugnant work involved digging up the more recent corpses, including Marion's mother and brothers. Having them exhumed so soon after their burials must have reopened the barely healed wounds of Marion's recent losses.

As Howe notes, while it was the valley's dead who were disturbed, it was the living who suffered "the pangs of heartache and loneliness" and who carried the memory of loss to their own graves.[167]

Chapter 13

THE WOODPECKERS DESCEND

L ike Marion, during the early years of the reservoir's construction,
Edwin Howe conducted his daily life and his commitments to
Enfield as he always had. He continued to serve as deacon and
trustee of the Congregational church and in various leadership roles at
the Bethel Lodge of Masons. His wife, Annie, also remained active in her
community roles, occasionally hosting meetings of the Women's Auxiliary of
the Congregational Church and the Quabbin Club at the Howe homestead.

Edwin and his son Ned also continued their management of the post
office on Main Street and the telephone exchange from Edwin's home on
Bridge Street. By the mid-thirties, the Howe store and post office was one of
the few remaining establishments on Main Street. With the other buildings
empty and boarded up and the railroad track and stations gone, the center of
Enfield looked more abandoned with each passing year. By 1935, Enfield's
population had dropped below five hundred people, and Greenwich, Dana
and Prescott combined had another five hundred residents.

The year 1936 ushered in a more intense and palpable phase of the
valley's destruction. The construction of the Enfield dam and the Greenwich
baffle dam began, and that summer, thousands of men from Boston arrived
to clear the valley. These young and inexperienced woodcutters were
charged with razing all vegetation within the thirty-eight square miles of the
watershed area, with a focus on the twenty-five thousand acres that would
lie below the eventual flood line. Massachusetts governor Curley used these
highly sought-after Depression-era jobs as a political tool, bestowing them

A group of "woodpeckers" in the summer of 1936. *Swift River Valley Historical Society.*

on the districts whose representatives supported him and his budget.[168] The men hired, a motley crew of former actors, boxers, athletes, musicians, electricians, bartenders, contractors and mechanics, referred to their place of work as Curley's Summer Camp.[169]

Valley residents quickly nicknamed the woodcutters "woodpeckers" because of their noisy, slow and inept work. It was clear to country folk that most of these men had never swung an axe or used a saw before. In addition to their inexperience, the woodpeckers were seen as lazy by valley residents like Doc Segur, who observed that "an ordinary man in the woods can cut three cords of wood a day. An exceptional woodsman can cut four or five cords. But one foreman told me he had a crew of thirty men in the woods for a week and they cut just eleven cords. That wood cost about $90 a cord."[170]

A *Springfield Republican* article entitled "Into the Valley of the Swift River Come 3,000 Men with Ax, Saw and Brush Hooks" noted that the valley got a whole lot louder that summer, as the "ring of ax and buzz of saw add a new note to the cadence of activity in the Swift River." The woodpeckers worked in groups of forty to forty-five scattered throughout the valley, chopping trees and brush and tossing branches into huge piles that resembled overgrown haystacks. On days when the fire hazard was low and the wind just right, the brush piles were burned, plumes of smoke billowing toward the valley's skies. Any sellable hardwood was shipped out; "long caravans of hardwood" wound over the roads that led away from the valley. All the valley's beautiful forests and the protective shade disappeared, replaced by naked "stumpy land"[171] that baked in the hot summer sun. The only wooded areas that remained were the hilltops, which would later become the reservoir's sixty islands.

Doc Segur tended to the woodpeckers' injuries, which in June 1936 were "remarkably slight and few,"[172] though in July, one man was killed by a falling tree. On June 27, a car packed with workers lost control on a corner in Ware and rolled four times before crashing into a tree. The driver died on his way to Mary Lane, and his eight passengers were admitted for care at the hospital.[173] As Doc Segur noted, "Nine out of 10 of [the woodcutters] had police records….They drove here in crowds every day, forcing people off the roads and causing many accidents. They caused a rise in the automobile insurance rate."[174]

Of the 3,000 woodpeckers who worked in the valley that summer, half of them lived in Ware, a town approximately eight miles away with a population of about 7,500.[175] Ware's police department was stretched thin that summer as the men worked in the valley by day and sought fun in Ware by night. There were many instances of public drunkenness, erratic driving, car accidents and other bad behavior, and some woodpeckers lost their jobs as a result.

Though Ware was far more bustling than the sleepy valley towns, it felt the 20 percent population increase that summer. Every woodpecker wore a button as identification, but they were not difficult to spot in any event. They made a spectacle each evening as they returned from their work in the valley, "rolling home in crowded autos and packed trucks" in "full regalia of lumberjacks."[176] They filled Ware's restaurants, stores, hotels and banks, which had to be kept open after hours on Wednesdays for the long lines of men waiting to cash their paychecks. There were reports of some Ware establishments upcharging the woodpeckers for food and rent, which were duly investigated.[177] Ware town officials worked with the metropolitan commission to provide entertainment for the men, creating a baseball league and scheduling boxing and tennis matches—anything to keep them busy and out of trouble.

Even within the ranks of the commission engineers, the woodpeckers were a cause for concern, and the engineers believed that they had to be closely watched. It was a relief to everyone when the chaos of that summer came to an end. By September, the clearing was 90 percent done, and many workers departed in November.[178] Approximately one thousand of the most committed stayed through December, though "the rigors of the weather had eliminated sluggards from the project."[179]

By the end of 1937, the woodpeckers had flown. Later, professional laborers would complete the clearing of the valley in the final phase of the project.

Chapter 14

Losing the Landmarks

While Ware's main street was booming, Enfield's was withering. Few main street establishments remained. The landmarks of the town hall, the Swift River Hotel and the Congregational church still stood, becoming more dilapidated with each passing year of neglect. In 1934, the Congregational church was sold to the commonwealth for $40,000, but it remained in use by the active members, who were preparing to celebrate its 150th anniversary in August 1936.

But on Saturday, August 1, just one week before the anniversary service, Enfield's stately and picturesque Congregational church—the most visible symbol of the valley's Puritan roots and "the pride of the inhabitants of the town, and much admired by visitors"—was burned to the ground. It was an act of arson that devastated the town and the valley.[180] The *Republican* reported that "the older residents, who have accepted even the loss of their homes with gentle fortitude, find the loss of their beautiful old church… almost unbearable."[181]

There were two different reports of the fire's discovery. One, in the *Republican*, was that the town constable, who also served as church janitor, was awakened at 4:20 a.m. by a passing stranger who said the town hall was on fire; one, in the *Globe*, was that Elliot Harwood, employed by postmaster Ned Howe, went to his automobile, which he kept in the church horse shed, at 4:30 a.m. and discovered the flames.

The fire was apparently set in the committee room in the northwest corner of the church and, fed by the wind, moved so quickly that the chapel and

Enfield Congregational Church on fire. *Swift River Valley Historical Society.*

nearby Haskell residence were also engulfed in flames before it could be put out at seven o'clock, three hours later. The nearby historic Joseph Hooker house and barn were also damaged. Enfield required the assistance of many local fire departments, including those of Ware, Athol, Belchertown, Dana, Barre and New Salem, to fight the blaze. The *Globe* put the total loss and damages of all structures at $117,000.[182]

Doc Segur immediately declared that the fire's origins were incendiary. The *Republican* reported rumors among valley residents that the fire was set by a disgruntled woodpecker, given that many had been recently discharged for bad behavior. That same day, several young men shouted from a passing automobile, "You haven't seen half of it yet; wait until next week!" This threat sent townspeople deeper "into a state of fear, bordering on panic."[183] They gathered on Enfield's common and watched anxiously as plainclothes policemen conducted their investigation. Guards were placed on all roads leading into the center of town, and they kept a record of all cars entering and leaving Enfield. Hundreds of motorists visited town on Sunday, August 2, many trying to get souvenirs of the burned church. Doc Segur, Leroy Hammond of the metropolitan commission and the state fire marshal launched investigations into the fire's origins. However, no culprits were ever identified.

Despite the loss of the church building, more than two hundred people attended the Congregational church anniversary service on Sunday, August 9, at the Masonic Lodge, followed by lunch in the town hall.[184] Reverend Curtis, by then retired, returned to pay tribute to the church and its membership. Letters were read from former pastors who could not attend, including Reverend Richards of the centennial, who wrote that he hoped to return but that "it is a serious wrench to the emotions to see such a 'deserted village.'"[185]

Reverend Randolph Merrill, son-in law of former Enfield minister Robert Woods, gave the address. He said of the loss of the church building, "Since it has gone up in flames, and since it was doomed soon to end its career in this place, may we not take some slight satisfaction in the thought that it is safe from possible desecration?" He concluded:

> Shall we not end on that note? Not many years remain for the Enfield church as a distinct organization. Soon there will be no Enfield either to need or to maintain a church. The last members will be scattered to other communities, taking their places in other churches. With thanksgiving as we look back, let us take courage as we look forward. Let us think that if the difficulties and discouragements of the remaining years are faced with faith and resolution, at the end the church of Enfield will not die, but will be living on in a host of lives throughout the world—and in Life Eternal.[186]

Though the church was completely lost to the fire, some of its objects were salvaged. The marble baptismal font was saved and later presented to the Granby church by Amanda Ewing's daughters, carrying out the wishes expressed by their mother before her death. The slightly melted bell that fell from the steeple during the blaze was also rescued. Marion had most of it recast into a smaller bell and mounted in the belfry of the Central Congregational Church of nearby New Salem. The remainder was recast into tiny silver dinner bells that served as mementos of the lost church for its scattered members.

The congregation continued to gather at the Enfield Grange for services. On June 26, 1938, the final service of the Congregational church was led by Reverend Burton Marsh. Then Reverend Curtis, returning once more from retirement, offered a prayer at the disbanding of the church community whose deep history had meant so much to its members, to the town of Enfield and to the greater Swift River Valley:

> *We thank thee, O Lord, for these hills, from whence our strength has come. We thank thee for the valleys that lie between the hills; and the streams and lakes that have brought life and beauty, recreation and industry to those who have dwelt here, and visitors from near and far. We thank thee for the countryside with its farms and fruit and fertility. We thank thee for the pleasant villages and hamlets scattered through this area. We thank thee for the homes that have meant so much to the people who have dwelt here; and, from which have gone many to gladden, bless and ennoble the world far and near. We are grateful for those who elected to stay in this valley and make its history. We are proud of their achievements and the things that they have inspired others to perform….We thank thee for those who have endured to the end, have not allowed religious services to cease nor faith to falter. And now, as we look to the future, may we not allow distrust to blind us or disappointment to embitter us, but may we, with the sublime faith of the Psalmist say; I will fear no evil for thou art with me. Amen.*[187]

In 1937, another Enfield landmark, the Swift River Hotel, was demolished. The hotel's landlord, William Galvin, had sold it to the state a decade earlier in 1927 but leased it and continued operations during the Quabbin's construction, hosting commission members and Boston politicians who visited the project. In November 1937, the building and adjoining barn and garage were purchased by a Chicopee man for $200, and the plumbing and heating apparatus was removed. Within three months, the hotel and its outbuildings were torn down, and the empty foundation of the once "neat and attractive" hotel now matched the specter of the Congregational church just across the street.[188]

As the town's landmarks disappeared, so, too, did its social organizations. The Order of the Eastern Star was disbanded on April 28, 1938. The Greenwich and Enfield Granges gave up their charters to the state organization and disbanded on June 16, 1938; the meeting was so crowded that the more than 350 attendees needed to relocate to the town hall. The remaining funds of the valley Granges assisted with the erection of a new Grange building at the Eastern States Exposition in Springfield.

Marion had remained a charter member of the Quabbin Club throughout its lifespan but had not been an active member for some time. However, on Tuesday, December 13, 1937, in what must have felt like a poignant bookend to her inaugural presidency, she hosted one of the final Quabbin Club meetings at Bonnieview.

The current club president, wife of engineer Jerome Spurr (one wonders what Marion thought of that), "expressed to Miss Smith the pleasure it gave to all of us to meet in her home—and to enjoy her cordial hospitality once more," according to the minutes. The meeting concluded with a social hour and refreshments prepared by Delia Tryon, which were "varied and delicious" and "served in the beautiful dining room."[189]

Marion did not attend the club's final meeting, held in Ludlow in May 1938, but she did surprise members with printed souvenir folders that included copies of Mary Cushman Hardy's poem "Quabbin Elegy."[190] Annie Howe was the only charter member of the club to attend. So ended the reign of Enfield's dominant social club, its members dispersed and its influence rendered irrelevant in a town destined to disappear completely.

Chapter 15

DISINCORPORATION

As Enfield headed into its final months, just over one hundred residents remained in town. Doc stayed active in many roles, including his all-consuming one as the valley's country doctor. He took on extra responsibilities, treating woodpeckers and dam and dike laborers for their injuries. And he continued to serve as medical examiner for the Fourth District of Hampshire County, attending many deaths and homicides.[191] Perhaps because he witnessed more tragedy than most, he was able to lead Enfield and the valley people through the towns' end-of-life experience with strength, grace and compassion.

The valley towns' date of disincorporation was April 28, 1938. Enfield held its final town meeting a few weeks earlier, on April 8. It took place in the town hall, which was originally slated for demolition on April 1, but remained standing because Enfield's children had to complete their school year and the building contained classrooms.

Doc, the chair of the board of selectmen, led the meeting during a terrible storm, "as snow and sleet beat against the windows…not unlike a death knell."[192] Marion, Edwin and Ned Howe were among the twenty-six residents present, along with a large number of reporters.

Doc Segur called the meeting to order, and Ned Howe was named moderator. The articles for consideration included a road machinery account and the sale of town property. The fifth and final article was to appropriate $1,800 to erect a monument "with a double message," to both honor Enfield's World War I veterans and "to commemorate the passing of this pre-revolutionary village."[193] Of Enfield, Doc Segur said, "We are proud of our town, and we are proud of our boys."[194] A committee of five was appointed to execute this monument to Enfield, including Doc Segur, Marion Smith and Edwin Howe.[195]

At the meeting's close, Enfield's town government dissolved.[196] Attendees remained afterward "to talk over the known past as well as the unpredictable future, perhaps realizing that before the $1,800 monument could be erected many of them would have long since joined their former townspeople in the Great Beyond, and their town almost entirely wiped off the face of the earth."[197] This retrospective comment by Donald Howe in *The Lost Valley* was telling. Doc's plan for a memorial never did come to pass—perhaps because three of the appointed committee members died within a few years of leaving the valley.

By mid-April, the end was drawing near. Many newspapers ran stories about the destruction of the Swift River Valley and the reservoir's construction, the articles sometimes sentimental, bordering on melodramatic.

The *Boston Globe* published a long front-page article about the valley on April 11, 1938, just a few days after Enfield's final town meeting (although it did not mention that event). It opened darkly:

> *It was a bad day for visiting Quabbin. The air was cold and the wind sharp. The grass looked as dead as it did before the Winter snows fell. Dead leaves hung upon the oaks. Even the evergreens looked dingy. Only in the swamps could one see signs of new life, in the lowly skunk cabbage and the faint green on little bushes. It was not a pleasant day in Spring, but it didn't make much difference to the people or to the valley itself. This is the last time Spring will ever come to Quabbin....When another April comes the waters will be rising in a dead world.*[198]

Seemingly in response to this grim dirge, just six days later, the *Springfield Republican* published its own front-page story about the valley's final days, which began by prompting readers toward empathy with the people still there: "What would you do, where would you go, how would you feel if you should be forced to vacate your homes, leave the land and community that has sheltered you all your life and given its best to support you, never to be able to return?"[199]

Both articles discussed the once vibrant valley's Puritan origins, Yankee grit and natural beauty, describing Enfield as "a thriving village, ideally situated, with a happy, contented and prosperous people, destined to an even more successful future."[200] They noted that Enfield was once among the richest towns in the commonwealth per capita but that in recent decades, "wealth dwindled, community spirit weakened"[201] and the valley's demise began. Since the 1920s, no new homes had been built, no new businesses established that might create jobs and resources. The *Republican* considered how difficult it would be for the businessmen of Enfield to transfer their businesses elsewhere, "to start again the long, laborious process of building up trade."

Both papers also addressed the sadness with which the older residents in particular were approaching their exile. The *Globe* suggested that some of them were taking their eviction "bitterly hard" and quoted Doc describing someone who could only be Marion Smith: "There is one woman whose ancestors were owners of the mills which brought wealth to them. They owned house and acres. Now the woman is 75 years old, last of her family alive. I don't know whether she will live two months longer....Her trouble is a broken heart."

While the *Globe*'s previous coverage of the Quabbin project had sometimes portrayed valley residents as slow or pedestrian, the *Republican* noted that "the people of Enfield and others in the area, who still maintain ownership rights in the district, cannot be termed 'diehards' or 'holdouts.' They are for the most part of above average intelligence with a true perception of values and an honest desire to be no more than properly compensated for the loss of their homes and business."

THEY WILL LOSE HOMES

TWO OF ENFIELD'S FIRST CITIZENS
Edwin H. Howe, 78, manager of town's 'phone exchange, hears Selectman Dr. Willard B. Segur tell how Quabbin waters will engulf town.

Both articles featured the same picture of Doc Segur and Edwin Howe. The *Republican* captioned it "Enfield's Leading Men Watch the Town Go Down," while the *Globe*, less respectfully, simply observed: "They Will Lose Homes."

The *Republican* wrote about the curiosity seekers and impertinent antiques collectors who descended on the valley, hoping to take home a relic of the lost towns. Marion was quoted as saying, "It's all anybody can do to keep a weathervane on a home or barn." And the reservoir laborers were also omnipresent, still tearing to pieces

Doc Segur and Edwin Howe, as featured in the *Globe* and the *Republican. Boston Globe archives, via Newspapers.com.*

"every tree, barn, home and shrub, representing years of work and security to someone," seemingly without knowledge or care "that they are wreaking more than physical devastation." On that note, the article described "numerous homes in different stages of dismantlement, some with the top floors and roofs lopped off," and the hills stripped bare of trees and brush up to the water line; only at that sight "does the thought really strike you that the road you are traveling will soon be under hundreds of feet of water."

Both newspapers tried to close on a positive note, by invoking progress. The *Globe* piece stated that

> *the dispossession of the dwellers in the Quabbin region is necessitated, of course, by the future need of the people of Greater Boston for water. The building of the great reservoir comes under the general head of progress, and some people suffer…so that people yet unborn may have good water to drink.*

These words would no doubt bring comfort to Boston readers. The *Springfield Republican* knew that its readership would feel differently and concluded by saying that the word *progress*, used by so many to describe the reservoir, was distasteful to valley residents who heard it used "by those who do not know the true, behind-the-scenes picture of the reservoir"—and who, because they did not live anywhere near the valley, probably never would.

Chapter 16

AULD LANG SYNE

A tear, hastily dried—a blare of dance music—voices—and
death came to Enfield.
—Associated Press, describing the Farewell Ball at midnight, April 27, 1938

The Farewell Ball, an event billed as a "a last good time for all," marked the valley towns' official disincorporation from the Commonwealth of Massachusetts 122 years after Enfield's incorporation and 184 years after Greenwich's. The Enfield Volunteer Fire Department spent their remaining $400 on the party—the same amount the town had initially appropriated for its centennial celebration. Doc Segur, again chairman of the planning committee, pulled out all the stops for this final social event, which harkened back to the firemen's balls once held annually. A decorator adorned the town hall "as never before,"[202] hanging black-and-white streamers from every corner, covering the casings of the broken windows in black and adding a "profusion of American flags" on the balcony and onstage. [203] Even the evening's programs were bordered in black, the same color worn by many of the residents for this occasion.

The evening was meant to begin with a parade, but too few firemen were available to form one.[204] Instead, a solitary old fire engine pulled by horses draped in black followed a band down Enfield's mostly boarded-up and abandoned main street. This funeral-like procession stopped in front of the dilapidated town hall, one of the very last structures still standing in town.

Farewell Ball interior decorations. *Swift River Valley Historical Society.*

Crowds of people streamed into the valley that evening, curious onlookers and press far outnumbering current and former valley residents. Hundreds of automobiles filled Enfield's otherwise empty streets and parked for more than a mile on either side of the town common. As at the centennial, Ware's police chief and four other officers were called in to help direct the traffic. It was difficult for those who purchased fifty-cent tickets to get inside the town hall that night. Although an estimated one thousand people filled the hall—far beyond its capacity—another one to two thousand walked around town or listened in from outside. Doc Segur had anticipated overcrowding and was "worried over the fact, although pleased to think so many have shown such interest and desire to attend."[205]

Doc, presiding over the town's truly final rite of passage, made remarks at the beginning of the evening. According to the *Republican*, "With noticeable difficulty the doctor referred to days that were to come when all who had been closely associated in community affairs would be scattered in new homes."[206] Women dabbed at their eyes with handkerchiefs and men fought back tears even as the night began, anticipating the emotion to come at midnight.

McEnelly's Orchestra, a ten-piece swing band from Springfield, kicked off the evening with a concert at eight o'clock, followed by a floor show by

The Grand March, led by Doc and Laura Segur (the man on Doc's left is McEnelly, leader of the orchestra). Photo by Arthur Griffin. *Griffin Museum of Photography.*

Springfield's Syner's dancing academy at eight thirty. At nine, the dancing began with the grand march led by Doc and Laura Segur, which wove its way through the grand hall.

People filtered in and out of the hall throughout the evening, heading to the Grange Hall across the street for ice cream, sandwiches and coffee— or to the town hall basement for free beer and other refreshments. The orchestra played old barn dance songs such as "Put on Your Old Gray Bonnet" and "Till We Meet Again," as well as the newer swing favorites for the younger crowd. Many reporters noted the gaiety of the young revelers, who danced all night and became so rowdy the hall began to shake. Meanwhile, the older folks sat in groups along the walls and in the balcony, talking of days gone by and reconnecting with former residents who had returned for this final evening, much as they had come back for the centennial twenty-two years before.

That evening, Marion Smith appeared at the ball in a black lace gown with a round star brooch at the center of her neckline. She wore a large corsage of white roses pinned to her right shoulder and a cascade of white ribbons on her left, with an opera-length string of pearls around her neck. The *Republican* captured several photos of her, and one of Marion with seven-year-old Marian Tryon made the front page the next day. In it, the two sit side by side, young Marian contrasting with her Nana in a white dress with matching bow pinned to her curled bob and a small rose corsage pinned on her left shoulder. They gaze at each other, their profiles to the camera, and the headline above them reads "Farewell to Enfield and Good Friends." Below, the caption reads,

> *Marion Agnes Tryon gazes up into the face of her namesake, Miss Marion A. Smith, as Enfield's firemen's ball Wednesday brought the end of a close relationship. Now that the town of Enfield is no more, these two, forced to move to other communities, will no longer enjoy daily meetings.*

This, of course, was not true, as anyone who lived in the valley knew. Marian Tryon would be moving together with Marion Smith in the near future. But even though the caption writer got his facts 100 percent wrong, he did capture the wrenching sense of impending loss valley residents were feeling.

Springfield Republican photo of Marion and Marian. *Swift River Valley Historical Society.*

Just before twelve, Doc Segur signaled the orchestra to stop playing. He called for a moment of silence for Enfield, Greenwich, Dana and Prescott. When the clock struck midnight, the orchestra began to softly play "Auld Lang Syne" in honor of the now deceased valley towns. As Howe wrote in *The Lost Valley*, "Muffled sobs could be heard from all parts of the hall, and many hardened men were noted making hurried grasps for their handkerchiefs. Children broke into tears as all realized this was the last gathering of its kind in Enfield, and for that matter, about the last affair of any kind to take place in the community."[207]

The orchestra played until two o'clock in the morning. The last song was "Home! Sweet Home!,"[208] a popular tune whose lyrics captured the feeling of the older residents in the town hall that evening:

> *'Mid pleasures and palaces*
> *Though I may roam*
> *Be it ever so humble*
> *There's no place like home*
>
> *A charm from the sky*
> *Seems to hallow us there*
> *Which seek thro' the world*
> *Is ne'er met with elsewhere*
>
> *Home! Home! Sweet, sweet home!*
> *There's no place like home*
> *There's no place like home!*[209]

Chapter 17

LEAVING HOME

The *Springfield Republican*'s lengthy article about the valley's last days, which ran ten days before the Farewell Ball, included interviews with Doc, Marion and the Howes about their plans for the future. At that point, they all made it clear that they wanted to hold on to their homes and possessions as long as possible. But when pressed, each revealed that they had been mulling over possibilities.

Of Edwin and Annie, the reporter noted that they

> *live in a comfortable home and had planned to spend their last days in comfort in the country they have come to know so well.…As others have done, they may move to Ware where they have a son, a successful businessman, but this is only one of many plans they have been considering.*

Similarly, Doc Segur

> *is willing to settle with the state and may also move to Ware where he is a member of the hospital staff. He has not yet sold out, but said that he was first propositioned by members of the Metropolitan District Water Supply commission only a few weeks ago.*

Doc had actually settled with the state in January but had not yet made definite plans to move to Ware.

Even the reserved Marion was willing to hint at what was in her mind at the time:

Miss Marion Smith, well-to-do, who lives in a beautiful home high above Smith's Village, has not yet closed any deal with the state but realizes that eventually she will have to leave and so has been searching for a new home. She has not yet found one with a view that matches the one from her large sitting room window where you can look across the valley to Great Quabbin.[210]

The night of the Farewell Ball marked not only the disincorporation of the valley towns but also the taking of the remaining valley lands of any residents who had not yet sold to the state. So the Howes, the Segurs and Marion, along with other Enfielders who attended the ball, returned after midnight to homes that no longer belonged to them and which now were part of Ware, because the boundaries of six surrounding towns shifted in the wake of the four towns' disappearance.[211]

R. Nelson Molt wrote to all remaining residents that next day: "You are hereby formally notified that the corporate existence of the aforesaid towns ceased at 12 o'clock midnight, April 27th." Marion's 274 acres of land and buildings were taken by eminent domain that evening. In October, she would agree to a settlement of $57,000 for that property. The Howes' 5.4 acres were also taken, and they later settled for $32,000 for their residential and commercial buildings and property. Doc had accepted the commission's offer of $26,500 for his property in January 1938, with the stipulation that he would remain in his home as long as possible.

Valley residents were allowed to stay through the conclusion of the school year but were expected to vacate their homes by July 1, 1938. But now that Enfield was no more and they would soon be evicted, the town's most prominent residents and last holdouts were forced to confront their final "sad and painful duty": they had to decide where to go.

Edwin and Annie Howe in their new home in Ware. *Personal collection of Edwin Howe's great-grandson Martin Howe.*

As it turned out, they all chose Ware, the place closest to their hometown and closest to each other. The Howes settled in a Victorian Foursquare house at 61 Church Street in Ware, joining their son Donald and his family in that town.[212] Ned, Enfield's postmaster, would follow later, the final resident to leave Enfield after the post office was closed in January 1939.

Doc and Laura purchased a Second Empire Victorian home at

67 Church Street, at the edge of the entrance to Grenville Park, just two houses down from Edwin and Annie, so the Howes and Segurs would be neighbors in Ware as they had been in Enfield. Doc had cards printed for his patients that announced his "removal" to Ware after June 20, 1938, and listed his office address as 45 Main Street.

In May 1938, Marion purchased a large piece of land on Highland Street in Ware—yes, on a hill—and decided to build a new home there, just a few blocks away from the Segurs and the Howes.

Marion stayed in Bonnieview until the summer, so Marian could complete her school year in the classrooms of the town hall. The school's final graduation took place on June 22, 1938, as two girls and five boys were awarded their grammar school diplomas by Doc Segur, who posed for a photo with the graduating class. The recessional, "Auld Lang Syne," was an echo from the Farewell Ball.

Edwin, Doc and Marion's last moments in Enfield are lost to us. We can imagine the sadness of their final days there, as they moved a lifetime's worth of belongings away from their beloved homes. They could still recall the once lush and vibrant Swift River Valley as it looked on a verdant July morning—as it did at the centennial—smelling of dew and fresh earth, the

Top: Howe home on Bridge Street in Enfield before the reservoir. *Personal collection of Edwin Howe's great-grandson Martin Howe.*

Bottom: Former location of Howe home on Bridge Street; note drainpipe by sidewalk for physical orientation. *Personal collection of Edwin Howe's great-grandson Martin Howe.*

Enfield's Main Street in ruins, circa 1938. *Swift River Valley Historical Society.*

white steeple of the Congregational church standing out against the green backdrop of Mount Ram. But now, as they departed, the view out the car windows would have looked like the aftermath of a disaster, a desolate landscape of gaping cellar holes, smoldering foundations and jagged tree stumps. Only the town hall still stood, a symbol of the valley's storied past, its own days numbered.

Bill Segur later recalled vividly the day he could no longer return to his Enfield home. His mother, Laura, had told him, "Bill, when you get home, get a ride to Ware because we just bought a house in Ware and we're going to move there." He remembered: "When I got back from work, in front of me was the place I had been born, and it was just a cellar hole. It was still burning. They'd burned it all day long.…That hit me pretty hard that day. I knew we were going to have to move, but I really enjoyed a childhood in that town."[213]

On the evening of July 11, an intense lightning storm with heavy hail swept through Enfield. Traffic came to a standstill, and power lines were blown down.[214] By July 14, just three families remained in Enfield. Soon they, too, departed, and the town was left behind, empty of all the men, women and children who had once called it home.

Epilogue

EXILE

Only death can remove the rankling sorrow
from the memories of the older residents.
—L.S. Bartlett in The Lost Valley

EVERYWHERE WAS SILENCE

On a beautiful sunny September day in 1938, the Metropolitan District Water Supply Commission held an auction at the Enfield town hall of items saved from the valley towns, including Enfield's brick town hall itself and a few other buildings. The bulk of the sale objects were things like schoolbooks and supplies, firefighting equipment, tools and other miscellany. Evelina Gustafson, a non-resident valley enthusiast and collector, wrote that walking through the lower floor of the town hall that day was like walking through a museum, though she believed the residents had either kept or already sold the most valuable valley antiques. She referred to one holdout who sounded a lot like Marion Smith: "an elderly lady who had not sold one piece of household goods accumulated over the years. She has had truckload after truckload moved to her new place of residence and will sell to no one."

The City Wrecking Company of Springfield bought the town hall for $550, but the many small items sold for very little. In her book about the valley, published in 1940, Gustafson describes her feelings of sadness as she drove home from the auction that afternoon "knowing that the death knell of this lovely, little countryside had now rung." Gustafston closes her account with the suggestion to the reader that "if, perchance, you drive by this body of water—pray pause and give a thought to those towns who gave up the ghost so that folk of the younger generation might have sufficient water to quench their thirst. Once thriving little communities, they now lie forgotten."[215]

An article about the auction described the eeriness of that late summer day, as "cellar holes yawned" and "half-wrecked roofless houses stood stark in an un-private display of fronts ripped off by wreckers....No bird sang, no dog barked, barnyards stood deserted. Spirals of blue-gray smoke pointed fingers skyward from brush heaps fired toward the bottom of the basin. Everywhere was silence."[216]

On September 21, 1938, a powerful hurricane struck New England. Nearly twelve inches of rain fell in five days, raising the level of the Swift River by fifteen feet at the dam. Amazingly, neither the dam nor the dike was damaged, but fifty million board feet of timber was blown down in the watershed area, which expedited the final clearing of the valley below the waterline. Loggers and bulldozers were hired to clear the remaining brush and remove any organic material from the reservoir floor. The timber was mostly salvaged and sold, which provided additional revenue for the project. The entire project ended up costing just $53 of the $65 million allocated for it, mostly due to the Depression's effect on costs and wages.

Last Day of Mailing

That winter, no one remained in Enfield except the engineers and postmaster Ned Howe. After selling his house to the state, Ned lived above his store in what was left of the Howe block, the half that included the central heating system having already been torn down. Ned had just a woodstove and blankets to warm himself, and he was eager to follow his family and move out of the valley.

On January 14, 1939, Enfield's last mail was taken to Athol, ending 116 years of the post office's operation. The final post included nearly three thousand pieces of mail, the largest in Enfield's history.[217] This was, in part, thanks to Ned's brother Donald, a stamp collector, who publicized the valley's last mailing to his fellow collectors and enthusiasts. Special envelopes with a drawing of the reservoir were printed—an imaginative rendering, since the landscape at the time bore no resemblance to the giant lake. The illustration,

Right: Ned Howe in front of the post office on the last day of mailing. *Personal collection of Edwin Howe's great-grandson Peter Howe.*

Below: Ned and Donald Howe on Enfield's last day of mail. *Swift River Valley Historical Society.*

printed on the envelope's left side, was labeled "site of the Quabbin Reservoir," and the names of the valley towns were printed below or next to the blue of the reservoir water. The commemorative postmark had the usual "Enfield, Mass" and "January 14, 1939" but included a line along the bottom of the envelope that read, "Last Day of Mailing."

Many former valley residents took the opportunity to send special mail through this last post, and members of the Tryon family received quite a bit of mail from friends and family that day. Aunt Kay got a letter from a man named Justin who wrote that he hoped to "help dear old Uncle Sam to be busy on the last day of his sojourn in the little town that soon would be nothing but a 'good long drink.'"

Marian Tryon received a letter from family friend Mrs. Cavanaugh with the wish that she would like her new school "as well as [she] liked Enfield." Her best friend, Marjorie Rowe, wrote, "Thought I would send you a letter in the last mail from Enfield. I am glad to see the snow. Now we can go sledding."

Marian wrote to her mother and father, "I am sending you a note as a souvenir of old Enfield." And her parents wrote, "Dear Tuda, This envelope will be a constant reminder of the happy days that we lived together in dear old Enfield remembering 'Nana,' Kay, Grandpa, Mother and Daddy."

Marion Smith also wrote to Delia and Earl on her light blue Bonnieview stationary, and to her namesake, she wrote, "Dear Tuda, Just a little note from Bonnieview and Enfield where you have passed so many happy hours to send love and good bye.—Nana."[218]

MORE GOODBYES

Doc Segur had little time to settle into life in his new home on Church Street in Ware. Although he had been very active during Enfield's final years, he must have been feeling unwell for some time before the wrenching move. By the fall of 1938, he'd become very ill, having developed a gangrenous ulcer in one leg, due perhaps to circulation problems or diabetes. He spent two months at the Deaconess Hospital in Boston, and his leg was amputated on January 4, 1939, in an effort to halt the infection. The surgery did not succeed. Doc died in Boston on January 27, 1939, at the age of seventy-three, just nine months after Enfield's life came to an end.

Doc's funeral was held on Sunday, January 29, 1939, at East Congregational Church in Ware, down the street from the Segur and Howe homes. An estimated one thousand people attended the funeral, and many mourners had to wait outside during the service to pay their respects. Hundreds of former valley residents attended, including Marion Smith and the Howes. Donald Howe was one of the honorary pallbearers.

Inside the church, more than one hundred floral pieces and wreaths surrounded the casket. According to a local newspaper, "Scores of women left the church following the solemn services wiping away tears and hard-bitten men folks whose families were cared for during the past years made little effort to hold back their feelings of genuine regret at losing their life-long friend."[219] At least three hundred automobiles followed the hearse into Ware's Aspen Grove Cemetery, where Doc's grave site was "piled high" with flowers and other tributes from friends, relatives and organizations.

The day after Doc's funeral in Ware, Quabbin's chief engineer, Frank Winsor, died suddenly in Boston. He collapsed of a heart attack on the stand at a Quabbin-related hearing while confirming his signature on a reservoir contract.[220] At the time of his death, Winsor was the highest-paid official in the commonwealth, even higher than the governor, with an annual salary of $13,500.[221] Seven hundred people attended his funeral on February 2 in West Newton, including many metropolitan commission engineers.[222] Just one day later, on February 3, 1939, the Metropolitan District Water Supply Commission voted to name the main Quabbin dam the Winsor Dam in memory of the chief engineer of the project from 1936 to 1939.[223]

Doc Segur's wife, Laura, lived on in the new house in Ware only two more years before dying in 1941 at age sixty-one and joining her husband in Aspen Grove Cemetery. Their neighbors down the street fared little better. In November 1942, Annie Howe passed away after a long illness. Three months later, eighty-three-old Edwin died also, following a short illness. They were buried in the new family plot at Mount Hope Cemetery in Belchertown. Their deaths occurred just a few months after the first waters from Quabbin began to flow through the aqueduct to the Wachusett Reservoir.

LIFE IN THE NEW HOUSE

Marion managed to make more of a life for herself in her new town. After leaving Enfield in the summer of 1938, she focused her energies on preparations for her new home on Highland Street. She chose Philip H. Rogers of Hardwick to design it, and as builder hired H.P. Cummings, a local construction company that had built a number of Ware landmarks, including the Mary Lane Hospital. The guaranteed contract to build the house was not to exceed $38,960, approximately $750,000 today.

During the year of construction, Marion, the Tryons and Aunt Kay lived on the Highland Street property in an existing Dutch Colonial home near the road. The house was small compared to the Enfield house, so she and her staff lived more like equals than mistress and servants.

Marion became very involved in the design and construction of her new home. Rumor had it that she first looked into moving Bonnieview in its entirety from Enfield. When that proved impossible, she settled for using parts of the old home in the new one. She had the builder remove trim, doors, flooring and the grand staircase from the Enfield house before it was destroyed, so she could integrate them into the Ware house.

Apparently, the builder found Marion's involvement to be challenging. H.P. Cummings's records indicate that "the owner demand[ed] changes almost every day," which ultimately cost $8,000 above the original quote—a nearly 15 percent cost overrun. The builder's records state that "final settlement with the owner was made on a toss of a coin basis and the only value of a detailed cost study would be to point at them as a shining example of what they should not be."[224]

The house's combination of new and older architectural elements created an interesting juxtaposition of styles. While its exterior and floorplan presented as a Colonial Revival, with a symmetrical layout and "modern" look and feel, the interior felt more Victorian, with tall, five-panel, solid wood doors and ornate brass hardware from the Queen Anne–style Enfield house. A *Ware River News* article noted that Marion wanted "each part of the interior of the Enfield home to be incorporated in the new home. As a result, many rare woods, such as Indian sycamore, now extinct, are contained in the Ware estate."

Marion intended the new house to be similar to Bonnieview in many ways. The main foyer looked nearly identical, similar in dimension and featuring the Enfield staircase; Marion even hung her brothers' portrait in the same location in both halls. Both houses were painted the same exterior colors, white with black shutters, and the cast-iron hitching post in the shape of a horse was placed by the porch. Like Bonnieview, the new property was planted with extensive flower gardens. Marion's gardener in Enfield, Jimmy Lisk, also moved to Ware and continued to work for her.

In another departure from social norms, Marion built the new house with rooms specifically designed for the Tryons. The symmetrical layout

Marion's new house in Ware. *Tryon family collection.*

allowed her to live on one side of the house while devoting the other side to the people who had become more like family than hired help to her. The Tryons' bedrooms, above the kitchen, included a bathroom and two adjoined bedrooms on the second floor. Marian Tryon's bedroom was the only one in the house with curtains, a wish of young Marian's that Marion Smith happily granted. The kitchen included a small dining area for the Tryons and a room off the kitchen that they used as a living room. On the third floor, Aunt Kay had her own bedroom and bathroom, and Marian Tryon had a playroom. The basement also served as a "rumpus room" for young Marian, who held birthday and Halloween parties there. All told, the Tryons probably occupied a larger portion of the fifteen-room house than Marion herself did.

By the time Marion and the Tryons moved into the house on July 11, 1939, their old hometown was a place of desolation. By then, even the town hall had been demolished. Just a month later, the valley completely empty of all life, the Quabbin Reservoir began to fill with water on August 14, 1939.

During her years on Highland Street, Marion mainly stayed at home. Marian Tryon could not recall her ever visiting the reservoir. Marion attended Ware's Congregational church on Sundays, where she might have seen Edwin and Annie Howe or Donald Howe with his family. She took occasional drives in her Rolls Royce, chauffeured by Earl, always with her lap robes to keep her warm. Marian Tryon remembered driving through tobacco fields on the way back from Hartford, Connecticut, one day, when

Enfield's town hall stands alone in the desolate valley, spring of 1939. *Department of Conservation and Recreation archives.*

Marion Smith looked out the window at a group of women working together in the fields and said, "I envy them." The younger Marian understood this to mean that Marion Smith envied their friendship and their community.

At home, Marion enjoyed listening to opera in her rocking chair beside the large living room fireplace, and she loved to hear Marian play on the Steinway from Enfield. After taking tea in the afternoons, Marion would rest in a small room that looked out over the gardens of the backyard. She would usually eat alone in the house's formal dining room, but from time to time, young Marian recalled, she would join the Tryon family for special meals at their small dining table in the kitchen.

Despite her advancing age, Marion's soft spot for her namesake was still in evidence. One winter, young Marian became very sick with pneumonia. During her weeks of illness, Marion would visit young Marian's bedroom with trays of jewels from her safe under the stairs, allowing her to play dress-up with her rubies and canary diamonds without leaving her sickbed.

In 1944, eighty-two-year-old Marion became ill. Sarah, the wife of Marion's cousin Albert Spitzli, had come to live with her around that time. "Cousin Sarah" slept in the bedroom near Marion's to assist in her care.

That year, Delia and Earl sent fourteen-year-old Marian to boarding school in Roxbury, Massachusetts, perhaps knowing that her Nana would soon pass away and not wanting young Marian to be present for her decline.

Marian Tryon received a letter from Cousin Sarah at school that fall saying that Marion was bedridden but had managed to walk the short distance to Sarah's room to ask her to write Marian to say she missed her.

Marion Smith died in her bedroom on November 6, 1944, of heart disease. The funeral services were held in her home, her body laid in front of the pocket doors from her Enfield home. She was later buried at Springfield Cemetery with her family, as she had planned.

Marion's death was headline news in western Massachusetts. Several local papers, including the *Ware River News* and the *Springfield Republican*,

Marian Tryon, circa 1939. *Tryon family collection.*

published articles about her life, death and estate, with headlines such as "Miss Marion A Smith Passes Away Here: Miss Marion Andrews Died at Her Beautiful Home on Highland Street Monday"[225] and "Late Miss Marion Smith Left Well Over One Million Dollars."[226] One article noted that Marion lived on Highland Street for five years before her death, "making as many friends and being as interested in the community as one could expect of a woman who had lived in another place for over 75 years."[227] The article also noted her generosity to many charities and wrote that "she would never permit anything to be said about her charitable activities, though much could be written now."[228] And finally, a prediction: "Her will when it is read should be most interesting."[229]

It was indeed. Marion had left enormous $127,000 bequests in cash to individuals and $206,000 to organizations. The *Ware River News* said it was "the kind of will people dream about, remembering everybody, especially her Enfield friends, since scattered by the state reservoir flood."[230] However, as one newspaper noted, Marion "made no provision for the future of her real estate, consisting of her beautiful new home in Ware and a block of apartments and houses in Springfield, nor is it believed she left any private directions about it at all."[231] This omission was noteworthy because she left very specific directions for everything else, from monetary contributions to gifts of specific artwork and jewelry to certain friends, cousins and other individuals. With no instructions about the house in Ware, it would be disposed of in the settlement of the estate, and the proceeds would go to her three executors, her longtime Ware attorney John H. Schoonmaker and her cousins Mabel Allen Haskell and Sarah Armstrong Spitzli.

While the executors made substantial money from Marion's estate, the Tryons received much smaller gifts. Marion left Delia a sapphire and pearl circle pin, along with $5,000 and any goods and dishes "as may be agreed upon between her and my executor or executors and the decision of the latter is to be final."[232] To young Marian, she left the money to buy "a good piano" and a string of gold beads. To Aunt Kay she left $3,000. To gardener Jimmy Lisk she left $2,000.

Marion also left money to Doc Segur's son, Bill, and other former Enfield residents. She gave many thousands of dollars to organizations as well, including the American Missionary Society and Piedmont College in Georgia, both related to her Woman's Missionary Association work in Enfield. She gave to many hospitals, including Mary Lane in Ware, Wing Memorial in Palmer, and Cooley Dickinson in Northampton. To Mary Lane she left $5,000, which was used to buy the hospital's first X-ray equipment. They called the X-ray room the Enfield room.[233]

In December 1944, Marion's estate was settled in Hampshire County probate court and officially valued at $1.3 million. The house and Marion's other real estate holdings would be auctioned off, and the proceeds would be divided by Schoonmaker, Haskell and Spitzli.

Schoonmaker allowed the Tryons to stay in the Highland Street house for the remainder of 1944. When they left, they took the few items Marion left to them and also purchased her dining table, credenza and Steinway piano. They also had to account and pay for many household items, including their own bedroom furniture and all the kitchen cookware. They moved to East Brookfield, about twelve miles from Ware, and opened a boardinghouse. Marian completed high school in the 1940s, during which time she got a corgi that she named Enfield Sunset, or "Sunnie" for short. She married Raymond Waydaka in 1950 and had three children. The Waydaka family lived in the East Brookfield home with Earl and Delia.

Nearly a year after Marion's death, on September 26, 1945, it was publicly announced that an auction would be held at Marion's house on Highland Street. At that time, Marion's estate was valued at $1.5 million, and the items included twenty-six Oriental rugs, household goods and many pieces of antique furniture. A local newspaper reported that "Sunday's auction will symbolize the passing of one of Massachusetts's most influential families."[234]

At an auction preview on Sunday, September 30, more than one thousand interested buyers and curious neighbors showed up to walk through Marion's home and rummage through her lifetime of belongings, which she had refused to sell while she was alive.[235] It is difficult to imagine that

Marion, a very private person during her life, would have appreciated such an intrusion, even after her death. That night, strong winds knocked over the auction tent, which was repaired the next morning.[236]

Attendance at the actual auction was much smaller; approximately three hundred people turned out to bid on Marion's personal effects. The items that sold for the highest prices were rugs, including her large living room rug, going for $1,250. Her grandfather clock fetched $250 and a silver set $300. Marion's many paintings were sold at below estimated value.[237]

With few friends and family members left to mourn her passing, Marion was remembered publicly as a generous woman of "broad interests and keen mind"[238] who bestowed her family's vast fortune among the people and institutions who meant so much to her during her lifetime. Even decades after the deaths of her grandfather, father and uncles, the Smith family's contributions to the Swift River Valley were remembered and celebrated at Marion's death. The Swift River Manufacturing Company was recalled as producing "nothing but the very finest pure woolens and relations between the Smith family and their workers were on a personal basis." Marion was described as "the last member of a family which had played a leading role in the economic development of New England for generations," and it was said that "many educational and charitable institutions throughout the country have been aided financially by the Smith family."[239]

Meanwhile, in 1944, the same year as Marion's death, the Winsor dam and the Goodnough dike of the Quabbin Reservoir opened to the public. And on June 22, 1946, the reservoir reached capacity, its waters poured over the spillway and the towns of the Swift River Valley were lost forever.

CHILDREN OF THE LOST VALLEY

The next generation of Enfield's most prominent citizens did not stray far from their lost valley. Doc's son, Bill Segur, settled in Ware with his wife and three children and operated a shoe store on Main Street for many years.

The Howes' youngest son, Milton, lived in West Springfield, where he was later joined by his brother Ned, while Donald remained in Ware. Donald was active in Ware's business and civic life, following his father's example. In addition to establishing the Ware Coupling and Nipple Company, where he served as president and treasurer, he also owned and operated the Quabbin Antique and Book Shop and the WARE Radio station.

In the late 1940s, a decade after valley residents' exodus, Donald announced on his radio station that he was compiling a book about the Swift River Valley's history and people, and he invited all former residents to submit their stories, articles and photos. He then worked to compile all the information he had gathered with some assistance from his brother, Ned. The result, published in 1951, was *The Lost Valley*, a six-hundred-page tome that continues to be the main archive of Swift River Valley material today. The book was illustrated by Donald's daughter Elizabeth "Betty" Howe Lincoln, a resident of Ware who taught art at Ware High School and was a prolific artist in her own right.

Donald dedicated *The Lost Valley* to "all the people of the Swift River Valley." In the preface, he wrote, "The Swift River Valley will never pass into oblivion in the minds of its former residents. It is principally for those people who cherish its memories that this has been written. May it bring to mind many happy thoughts of lost days!"[240]

Marian Tryon Waydaka and her family continued to live in the Tryons' East Brookfield home for her entire life. In 2019, she visited Marion Smith's house in Ware for the last time. We walked the first-floor rooms together while she shared memories of her Nana, Enfield and her brief time in Ware. It meant a great deal to her to visit the house again, though some memories were painful to recall. Marian died in March 2021 at the age of ninety.

QUABBIN ELEGY

By Mary Cushman Hardy for the Quabbin Club

I am not dying, new life is mine;
Great Honor has come to me,
For high and low shall drink of my wine
In the vintage of memory.

My time is coming, but not quite yet,
My jewels I've sent to be re-set;
And the hills my sparkling wine shall find,
For I am the cup-bearer of all mankind.

The sun shall fling his crimson robe
Across my waters clear,
And the amber of the soft moonlight
Shall guide the timid deer.

The little creatures of the wood
Shall come and visit, where
The friendliness of solitude
Shall spread the mantle rare.

And when on bended knee I raise
My cool and jeweled cup,
If the waters lower 'neath its brim
The gods shall fill it up.

The gods of snow and ice and rain,
The gods of the slumbering hills,
The gods who take and give again,
Who grind their shadowing mills.

But say not death has come to me,
Beauty, not dust, you'll find;
For I stand among my towering hills,
Cup-bearer to all mankind.

NOTES

Preface

1. Marian Tryon Waydaka was named Marion at birth but changed the spelling to Marian as a young adult because she preferred what she believed was the more feminine spelling. I refer to her as Marian throughout the book.
2. Nipmuc Nation, "Brief Look at Nipmuc History."
3. Pulsipher, *Swindler Sachem*.
4. Kiley, Terry and Wikander, *Hampshire History*, 215.
5. Faludi, "America's Guardian Myths."
6. Ewing, "Enfield's History" and Underwood, *Quabbin*, 28.
7. Johnson, *Historic Hampshire*, 251.

Prologue

8. Greene, *Four Quabbin Towns Died*, 48.
9. *Ware River News*, "Miss Smith of Enfield."
10. Waydaka, interview by the author.
11. Philips, interview by Audrey Duckert.
12. *Boston Globe*, "Enfield Sadly Greets Spring."
13. Howe, *Lost Valley*.
14. Segur, oral history interview.
15. *Springfield Union*, "The Doctor."

Chapter 1

16. *Boston Globe*, "Enfield Preparing."
17. Ibid.
18. *Athol Transcript*, "Enfield's Fine Celebration."

19. Ibid.
20. Townsend, letter to Donald W. Howe.
21. *Boston Globe*, "Enfield Preparing."

Chapter 2

22. Underwood, *Quabbin*, 3–4.
23. Conuel, *Quabbin*, 3–4.
24. Underwood, *Quabbin*, 4.
25. *Springfield Republican*, "Town Centennial." (Richards's sermon was published in full in this article.)
26. Ibid.
27. *Athol Transcript*, "Enfield's Fine Celebration."
28. *Springfield Republican*, "Centennial."
29. Everts, *History of the Connecticut Valley*, 536.
30. Ibid.
31. Underwood, *Quabbin*, 27.
32. Rosenberg, *Before the Flood*, 1.
33. Ewing, "Enfield's History."
34. Johnson, *Historic Hampshire*, 251.
35. Everts, *History of the Connecticut Valley*, 537.
36. Johnson, *Historic Hampshire*, 222.
37. Ibid., 262.
38. Ibid., 101.
39. Underwood, *Quabbin*, 7.
40. Clark, *Quabbin Reservoir*, 32.
41. Howe, *Lost Valley*, 117.
42. Enfield Congregational church records.
43. Ibid., 122.
44. Woman's Missionary Society reports, Enfield section of the *Springfield Republican*.
45. Howe, *Lost Valley*, 103.
46. Enfield's Annual Reports.
47. Howe, *Lost Valley*, 182.
48. According to School Committee Reports in Enfield's Annual Reports: in 1891, the report noted that 109 boys and 80 girls were enrolled in Enfield schools; in 1892, 126 boys and 91 girls; in 1894, 127 boys and 104 girls; and by 1895, the numbers had evened out, to 106 boys and 106 girls.
49. Enfield's Annual Reports.

Chapter 3

50. *Springfield Republican*, "Hold Dedication."
51. Howe, *Lost Valley*, 149.

52. *Springfield Republican*, "Hold Dedication."
53. *Boston Globe*, weather report, July 4, 1916.
54. *Springfield Republican*, "Hold Dedication."
55. Ibid.
56. Underwood, *Quabbin*, 101.
57. Ewing, "Enfield's History."
58. Underwood, *Quabbin*, 122.
59. *Ware River News*, "Enfield."
60. Howe, *Lost Valley*, 186.
61. Kiley, Terry and Wikander, *Hampshire History*, 223.
62. Howe, *Lost Valley*, 187.
63. Ibid.
64. Ibid.
65. Ibid., 175.
66. *Springfield Republican*, "Death of a Prominent Enfield Man."
67. *Ware River News*, "Enfield."
68. *Springfield Republican*, "Death of Prominent Business Man."
69. Swift River Company advertisement booklet.
70. *Springfield Republican*, "Swift River Plant Sold."
71. Greene, *Quabbin's Railroad*, 171.
72. *Springfield Union*, "The Doctor."
73. Baystate Health, "History of Baystate Medical Center."
74. *Springfield Union*, "The Postmaster."
75. Underwood, *Quabbin*, 13–14.
76. *Enfield's Centennial Program*, "Howe's Handy Household Want Card."
77. Howe, *Lost Valley*, 90.
78. Ibid., 104.
79. Ibid.

Chapter 4

80. Theroux, "Enfield Gala Theatre."
81. Underwood, *Quabbin*, 362.
82. Greene, *Creation of the Quabbin*, 7.
83. Underwood, *Quabbin*, 269.
84. Greene, *Creation of the Quabbin*, 7.
85. Rosenberg, *Before the Flood*, 60.
86. Quabbin Club minutes, Swift River Valley Historical Society.
87. *Springfield Union*, "The Quabbin Club."
88. Howe, *Lost Valley*, 139.
89. Segur, Fireman's Association Correspondence.

Chapter 5

90. *Athol Transcript*, "Enfield's Fine Celebration."
91. Ibid.
92. Ibid.
93. Powers, "A 'Horribles' Parade."

Chapter 6

94. Howe, *Lost Valley*, 6.
95. Nesson, *Great Waters*, 1.
96. Rawson, *Eden on the Charles*, 13.
97. Clarke, *Boston's Golden Age*, 69.
98. Murphy, *Water for Hartford*, 249.
99. Nesson, *Great Waters*, 5.
100. Savage, "Water Works."
101. These new reservoirs included Sudbury, Whitehall, Hopkinton, Ashland, Stearns, Brackett and Foss.
102. Nesson, *Great Waters*, 13.

Chapter 7

103. Massachusetts State Board of Health, *Metropolitan Water Supply*.
104. According to Nesson in *Great Waters*: Arlington, Belmont, Boston, Brookline, Cambridge, Chelsea, Everett, Hyde Park, Lexington, Lynn, Malden, Medford, Melrose, Milton, Nahant, Newton, Quincy, Revere, Saugus, Somerville, Stoneham, Swampscott, Wakefield, Waltham, Watertown, Winchester, Winthrop and Woburn.
105. Massachusetts State Board of Health, *Metropolitan Water Supply*.
106. *Wachusett* is an Algonquin word meaning "near the mountain."
107. *Boston Globe*, "Living Death."
108. Nesson, *Great Waters*, 30.
109. Koren, *Boston 1822–1922*, 99.
110. *Boston Globe*, "Money for Many People."

Chapter 8

111. Steuding, *Handmade Dams*, 81.
112. *Springfield Republican*, "New York Water Works."
113. *Springfield Republican*, "Fifteen Men Killed."
114. *Springfield Union*, "Searchlight."
115. Clark, *Quabbin Reservoir*, 3.
116. Ibid., 4.

117. *Boston Globe*, "Goodnough Kept Fighting."
118. *Springfield Republican*, "Boston's Plan."
119. Abstract from the Report, 11.
120. Ibid.
121. Ibid., 5.
122. Ibid.,18.
123. *Boston Globe*, "$50m Project."
124. *Springfield Republican*, "Boston's Plan."

Chapter 9

125. *Springfield Republican*, "Hundreds Attend Hearing."
126. *Springfield Republican*, "Voice Strong Opposition."
127. Ibid., 8.
128. *Springfield Republican*, "Hundreds Attend Hearing."
129. Ibid., 1.
130. *Boston Globe*, "Urge Prompt Action."
131. Nesson, *Great Waters*, 50.
132. *Boston Globe*, "Would Take Sudbury."
133. Nesson, *Great Waters*, 52–53.
134. Ibid., 54.
135. Ibid., 59.
136. *Boston Globe*, "Thirsty Boston."
137. *Boston Globe*, "Quick Shift in Water Lineup."
138. *Boston Globe*, "Senate Amends Water Measure."
139. *Springfield Republican*, "Sharp Attacks."
140. *Boston Globe*, "Doomed Towns."

Chapter 10

141. *Springfield Republican*, "Swift River Valley Lives in Suspense."
142. *Springfield Republican*, "Boston Arranges."
143. *Boston Globe*, "Blast at Rutland."
144. Rosenberg, *Before the Flood*, 51–52.
145. Ibid., 44. For more information about the engineers, see *Before the Flood*, in which Rosenberg chronicles the many fascinating details of the reservoir's construction.
146. *Boston Globe*, "Quabbin, Massachusetts."
147. Segur, oral history interview.
148. Howe, *Lost Valley*, 240.
149. Ibid.
150. Ibid.
151. *Springfield Republican*, "Boston Arranges."
152. *Springfield Republican*, "Swift River Valley."
153. Ibid.

Chapter 11

154. *Springfield Daily News*, "Enfield."
155. Tryon, Delia, Marian Tryon's baby book.
156. Smiths, note to Delia Tryon.
157. Delia's salary was $1,500 twelve years later, according to the 1940 census.
158. Waydaka, interview with the author.
159. *Springfield Republican*, "Old Mill at Smith's."

Chapter 12

160. *Springfield Republican*, "Host of Swift River Valley Dead."
161. Cemetery Hill records.
162. Rosenberg, *Before the Flood*, 118, referencing letter from R. Nelson Molt to Woodlawn Cemetery custodian Frank L. Gage, August 25, 1932, quoting decision of August 2, 1932, Massachusetts State Archives.
163. Smith, letter to N. Leroy Hammond.
164. Rosenberg, *Before the Flood*, 120.
165. Segur, oral history interview.
166. *Springfield Republican*, "Quabbin Park."
167. Howe, *Lost Valley*, 233.

Chapter 13

168. *Ware River News*, "Gov. Curley Controls."
169. *Springfield Republican*, "Into the Valley."
170. Ibid.
171. Ibid.
172. Ibid.
173. *Boston Sunday Post*, "Crash Kills Roxbury Man."
174. *Boston Globe*, "Enfield Spring Flooding."
175. *Springfield Republican*, "Men with Ax."
176. Ibid.
177. *Worcester Gazette*, "Ware Officials Deny" and "Ware Area Prices."
178. *Ware River News*, "Trying to Find More Work."
179. *Worcester Telegram*, "1000 Still Working."

Chapter 14

180. *Springfield Republican*, "Old Enfield Church."
181. Ibid.
182. *Boston Globe*, "Enfield Incendiary."
183. *Springfield Republican*, "Enfield Folk Fear-Ridden."

184. *Springfield Republican*, "Old Enfield Church."

185. Order of Service, One Hundred and Fiftieth Anniversary.

186. Ibid.

187. *Ware River News*, cited in Greene, *From Valley to Quabbin*, 45.

188. *Springfield Republican*, "Old Swift River Hotel."

189. Quabbin Club minutes.

190. "Woman's Club."

Chapter 15

191. The *Globe* reported Segur's examinations of a number of deaths between 1927 and 1938: a priest who died in his sleep of a heart attack in 1931, a Boston man who accidentally drowned in Curtis Pond in Greenwich in 1932, a ten-year-old boy who was fishing a stream in Ware when a bridge collapsed on him in 1936, six young people in a car accident in Ware that left four women dead and two men seriously injured in 1937 and many others.

192. *Boston Herald*, "Soon to be Engulfed."

193. Ibid.

194. Ibid.

195. Howe, *Lost Valley*, 234.

196. Ibid.

197. Ibid., 235.

198. *Boston Globe*, "Sadly Greets Spring."

199. Neville, "Holds Heartaches."

200. Ibid.

201. *Boston Globe*, "Sadly Greets Spring."

Chapter 16

202. *Springfield Republican*, "Fireman's Ball."

203. *Springfield Republican*, "Enfield Will Hold Farewell Ball."

204. Greene, *Four Quabbin Towns Died*, 42.

205. *Springfield Republican*, "Enfield Will Hold Farewell Ball."

206. *Springfield Republican*, "Enfield's History Ends."

207. Howe, *Lost Valley*, 238.

208. Greene, *Four Quabbin Towns Died*, 46.

209. Ballad of America, "Home! Sweet Home!" This song was composed by Sir Henry Bishop, with lyrics adapted from John Howard Payne's 1823 opera *Clari*. The song was popular throughout the United States during the Civil War. Notable recordings include those by Vera Lynn (1941) and Bing Crosby (1945).

Chapter 17

210. *Springfield Republican*, "Holds Heartache."
211. These towns are New Salem, Petersham, Hardwick, Ware, Belchertown and Pelham.
212. Brown, scrapbook clipping.
213. Segur, oral history interview.
214. *Springfield Daily News*, "Heavy Hail, Lightning."

Epilogue

215. Gustafson, *Ghost Towns*, 125.
216. *Christian Science Monitor*, "Relics of Former Glory."
217. *Springfield Republican*, "Enfield Post Office."
218. Last post letters.
219. *Ware River News*, "Notable Tribute Paid."
220. *Boston Globe*, "Frank E. Winsor Dies."
221. Ibid.
222. *Boston Globe*, "Frank E. Winsor."
223. *Boston Globe*, "Quabbin Main Dam Named."
224. Cummings records.
225. *Ware River News*, "Miss Marion A. Smith."
226. *Ware River News*, "Late Miss Marion Smith."
227. *Ware River News*, "Miss Marion A. Smith."
228. Ibid.
229. Ibid.
230. *Ware River News*, "Leaves Generous Bequests."
231. Ibid.
232. Smith, will.
233. *Ware River News*, "$5000 Bequest."
234. *Ware River News*, "Antique Buyers."
235. *Ware River News*, "Smith Auction Highly Successful."
236. Ibid.
237. Ibid.
238. *Ware River News*, "Miss Marion A. Smith."
239. *Ware River News*, "Antique Buyers."
240. Howe, *Lost Valley*, viii.

BIBLIOGRAPHY

Books and Periodicals

Almquist, Frank. *Building the Ashokan Reservoir*. Charleston, SC: Arcadia Publishing, 2021.

Burk, John. *Quabbin Reservoir through Time*. Charleston, SC: Arcadia Publishing, 2014.

Clark, Walter E. *Quabbin Reservoir*. Athol, MA: Athol Press, 1994.

Clarke, Ted. *Beacon Hill, Back Bay and the Building of Boston's Golden Age*. Charleston, SC: The History Press, 2010.

Conuel, Thomas. *Quabbin: The Accidental Wilderness*. Brattleboro, VT: Stephen Greene Press, 1981.

Everts, Louis H. *History of the Connecticut Valley in Massachusetts*. Philadelphia: Louis H. Everts, 1879.

Greene, J.R. *B.V. Brooks's Pre-Quabbin Art, Photos & Postcards*. Athol, MA: Highland Press, 2014.

———. *The Creation of the Quabbin Reservoir: The Death of the Swift River Valley*. Athol, MA: Transcript Press, 1981.

———. *The Day the Four Quabbin Towns Died*. Athol, MA: Transcript Press, 1985.

———. *From Valley to Quabbin: 1938–1946*. Athol, MA: Athol Press, 2010.

———. *Quabbin's Railroad: The Rabbit*. Athol, MA: Highland Press, 1985.

Gustafson, Evelina. *Ghost Towns 'Neath the Quabbin*. Boston: Amity Press, 1940.

Howe, Donald. *Quabbin: The Lost Valley*. Ware, MA: Quabbin Book House, 1951.

Johnson, Clifton. *Historic Hampshire in the Connecticut Valley*. Springfield, MA: Milton Bradley, 1932.

Kiley, Mark, Helen Terry and Lawrence Wikander. *The Hampshire History: Celebrating 300 Years of Hampshire County, Massachusetts*. Northampton, MA: Hampshire County Commissioners, 1964.

Koren, John. *Boston 1822–1922 One Hundred Years a City: The Story of Its Government and Principle Activities*. Boston: City of Boston Printing Department, 1923.

Lepore, Jill. *The Name of War: King Philip's War and the Origins of American Identity*. New York: Vintage Books, 1999.

Murphy, Kevin. *Water for Hartford: The Story of the Hartford Water Works and the Metropolitan District Commission*. Wesleyan, CT: Wesleyan University Press, 2010.

Nesson, Fern L. *Great Waters: A History of Boston's Water Supply*. Hanover, NH: University Press of New England, 1983.

Peirce, Elizabeth. *The Lost Towns of the Quabbin Valley*. Charleston, SC: Arcadia Publishing, 2003.

———. *Quabbin Valley Life As It Was*. Charleston, SC: Arcadia Publishing, 2014.

———. *Quabbin Valley People and Places*. Charleston, SC: Arcadia Publishing, 2006.

Pulsipher, Jenny Hale. *Swindler Sachem*. New Haven: Yale University Press, 2018.

Rawson, Michael. *Eden on the Charles: The Making of Boston*. Cambridge, MA: Harvard University Press, 2010.

Roberts, George S. *Historic Towns of the Connecticut River Valley*. Schenectady, NY: Robson & Adee, 1906.

Rodgers, Daniel T. *As a City on a Hill: Boston's Most Famous Lay Sermon*. Princeton, NJ: Princeton University Press, 2019.

Rosenberg, Elisabeth C. *Before the Flood: Destruction, Community and Survival in the Drowned Towns of the Quabbin*. New York: Pegasus Books, 2021.

Seaholes, Nancy S. *Gaining Ground: A History of Landmaking in Boston*. Cambridge, MA: MIT Press, 2003.

Steuding, Bob. *The Last of the Handmade Dams: The Story of the Ashokan Reservoir*. Fleischmanns, NY: Purple Mountain Press, 1985.

Tougias, Michael. *Quabbin: A History and Explorer's Guide*. Yarmouth Port, MA: On Cape Publications, 2002.

Underwood, Francis Henry. *Quabbin: The Story of a New England Town*. Boston: Lee and Shepard, 1893.

Archives and Collections

Digital Commonwealth, accessed via https://www.digitalcommonwealth.org/.

Forbes Library's Quabbin Collection, Northampton, MA.

Friends of Quabbin materials shared by Gene Theroux.

Massachusetts Department of Conservation and Recreation's Collection at the Quabbin Visitor's Center, Belchertown, MA.

State Library of Massachusetts, accessed via https://archives.lib.state.ma.us/.

Stone House Museum, Belchertown, MA.

Swift River Valley Historical Society, New Salem, MA.

Tryon Family Collection shared by Mark Waydaka.

University of Massachusetts Special Collections, Amherst, MA.

Ware Young Men's Library, Ware, MA.

Archival Sources, Oral Histories and Interviews

Brown, Nellie. Scrapbook clipping. Collection of the Stonehouse Museum.

Cemetery Hill records. Collection of the Swift River Valley Historical Society.

Cummings, H.P. Records, contract #1114. Provided via email.

Enfield Congregational church records. Enfield (MA) Collection at the University of Massachusetts's Robert S. Cox Special Collections & University Archives Research Center.

Enfield's annual reports. Enfield (MA) Collection at the University of Massachusetts's Robert S. Cox Special Collections & University Archives Research Center.

Ewing, Amanda. "A Sketch of Enfield's History," in Enfield's Centennial Program, Enfield (MA) Collection at the University of Massachusetts's Robert S. Cox Special Collections & University Archives Research Center.

"Howe's Handy Household Want Card." Enfield (MA) Collection at the University of Massachusetts's Robert S. Cox Special Collections & University Archives Research Center.

Last post letters. Collection of the Tryon family.

Order of Service of the One Hundred and Fiftieth Anniversary of the Congregational Church. Collection of the Swift River Valley Historical Society.

Peirce, Elizabeth. Letter to the author on behalf of the Swift River Valley Historical Society, July 28, 2016.

Philips, Alice Twible. Interview by Audrey Duckert. In *Audrey R. Duckert Quabbin Valley Oral History Collection, 1966–1980*, accessed via the University of Massachusetts's Robert S. Cox Special Collections & University Archives Digital Collection.

Quabbin Club minutes. Collection of the Swift River Valley Historical Society.

Segur, Bill. Oral history interview. Accessed via Dropbox from Friends of Quabbin.

Segur, Willard B. Fireman's Association correspondence, September and October 1915. Enfield (MA) Collection at the University of Massachusetts's Robert S. Cox Special Collections & University Archives Research Center.

Smith, Marion. Will. Accessed at the Hampshire County Probate Court in Northampton, MA.

Smith, Marion. Correspondence with N. Leroy Hammond, August 19, 1935. Enfield Cemetery records at the Massachusetts Department of Conservation and Recreation, located at the Quabbin Visitor's Center.

Smiths. Note to Delia Tryon, 1928. Tryon family collection.

Swift River Company advertisement booklet, 1912. Collection of the Swift River Valley Historical Society.

Townsend, H.E. Letter to Donald W. Howe regarding Enfield's Centennial, March 3, 1916. Enfield (MA) Collection at the University of Massachusetts's Robert S. Cox Special Collections & University Archives Research Center.

Tryon, Delia. Marian Tryon's baby book. Tryon family collection.

Waydaka, Marian Tryon. Interview with the author, Ware, Massachusetts, March 13, 2019.

Woman's Missionary Society reports. Enfield (MA) Collection at the University of Massachusetts's Robert S. Cox Special Collections & University Archives Research Center.

Newspapers and Periodicals

Boston Globe archives. Accessed via https://www.newspapers.com.

Journal of the New England Water Works Association Archives. Accessed via https://newwa.org/Publications/TheJournalandArchives.aspx.

Springfield (MA) Republican archives. Accessed via masslive.newsbank.com.

Springfield (MA) Union archives. Accessed via masslive.newsbank.com.

Ware (MA) River News archives. Accessed at Ware River News, 80 Main Street, Ware, Massachusetts.

Articles

"Abstract from the Report of the State Department of Public Health and the Metropolitan District Commission Upon the Water Supply Needs and Resources of the Commonwealth." Boston: Wright & Potter Printing, 1922.

Athol (MA) Transcript. "Enfield's Fine Celebration: One Hundredth Anniversary Beautifully Observed." July 11, 1916, 1. Collection of the Swift River Valley Historical Society.

Ballad of America. "Home Sweet Home: About the Song." Accessed July 16, 2022. https://balladofamerica.org/home-sweet-home/.

Bashour, Mark J., and Delphis L. Levia Jr. "Interpreting the Place Space of an Extinct Cultural Landscape: The Swift River Valley of Central Massachusetts." *Historical Journal of Massachusetts* 34, no. 2 (Summer 2006): 149–70.

Baystate Health, "History of Baystate Medical Center." Accessed January 22, 2022. https://blog.choosebaystatehealth.org/the-history-of-baystate-medical-center.

Binder, Rebecca. "Quabbin: Land of Many Waters." *Amherst Magazine* (Spring 2006). https://www.amherst.edu/amherst-story/magazine/.

Boston Globe. "Blast at Rutland Opens Shaft in First Operation of New Water Supply Project." May 12, 1927.

———. "Doomed Towns Ask Swift End." February 4, 1927, 8.

———. "Enfield Incendiary $117,000 Fire." August 1, 1936.

———. "Enfield Preparing for Its 100th Birthday." June 18, 1916.

———. "Enfield Sadly Greets Spring as Quabbin Flooding Nears." April 11, 1938.

———."$50m Project to Prevent Water Famine in Next Five Years." January 27, 1921.

———. "Frank E. Winsor." February 3, 1939.

———. "Frank E. Winsor Dies on Witness Stand." January 31, 1939.

———. "Goodnough Kept Fighting for His Water Supply Plan." May 31, 1926.

———. "Living Death That West Boylston Is Enduring, Eloquent Plea in Town's Behalf." February 27, 1895.

———. "Money for Many People: Nearly Everybody in Boylston, Sterling and Clinton Gets Something from the State Because of the Wachusett Reservoir—About $350,000 Have Already Been Paid." November 22, 1903.

———. "Quabbin Main Dam Named for Winsor." February 4, 1939.

———. "Quabbin, Massachusetts 65 Million Dollar Baby." Probably 1936. Clipping in the collection of the Swift River Valley Historical Society.

———. "Quick Shift in Water Lineup: Goodnough Plan Likely of Adoption This Week to End Long Discussion of Metropolitan Supply." May 10, 1926.

———. "Sadly Greets Spring as Quabbin Flooding Nears." April 11, 1938.

———. "Senate Amends Water Measure." May 18, 1926.

———. "Thirsty Boston." October 7, 1925.

———. "Urge Prompt Action on $60,000,000 Water Plan." May 23, 1922.

———. Weather report. July 4, 1916.

———. "Would Take Sudbury and Assabet Rivers." October 16, 1925.

Boston Herald, "Soon to Be Engulfed for Reservoir, Enfield Holds Last Town Meeting." April 9, 1938.

Boston Sunday Post, "Crash Kills Roxbury Man." June 28, 1936.

Christian Science Monitor. "Relics of Former Glory Put on Block by Deserted Village." September 11, 1938. Clipping at UMass Special Collections.

Faludi, Susan. "America's Guardian Myths." *New York Times*, September 7, 2007. https://www.nytimes.com/2007/09/07/opinion/07faludi.html.

Massachusetts Department of Recreation and Conservation. *Reading the Land: Massachusetts Heritage Landscapes, a Guide to Identification and Protection*. https://www.mass.gov/doc/reading-the-land-massachusetts-heritage-landscapes-a-guide-to-identification-and-protection/download.

———. *Terra Firma: Putting Historic Landscape Preservation on Solid Ground*. https://www.mass.gov/doc/terra-firma-putting-historic-landscape-preservation-on-solid-ground/download.

Massachusetts State Board of Health, *Report […] Upon a Metropolitan Water Supply, February, 1895*. Boston: n.p., 1895.

Massachusetts Water Resources Authority. "Metropolitan Boston's Water System History." https://www.mwra.com/04water/html/hist1.htm.

Neville, Paul. "Quabbin Reservoir Holds Heartaches for Swift River Valley as Deadline Looms." *Springfield (MA) Republican*, April 17, 1938.

New York City Environmental Protection. "History of New York City Drinking Water." https://www1.nyc.gov/site/dep/water/history-of-new-york-citys-drinking-water.page.

Nipmuc Nation. "Brief Look at Nipmuc History." Accessed January 22, 2021. https://www.nipmucnation.org/our-history.

Powers, Matthew. "A 'Horribles' Parade." Woodstock History Center. Accessed July 16, 2022. https://www.woodstockhistorycenter.org/articles/ahorribleparade?rq=horribles.

Rosenberg, Elisabeth C. "Building the Dams That Doomed a Valley." MIT Technology Review, June 29, 2021. https://www.technologyreview.com/2021/06/29/1025739/building-the-dams-that-doomed-a-valley/.

Savage, Neil J. "Water Works—After the Celebration." *Boston Globe*, June 20, 1981.

Springfield (MA) Daily News. "Enfield." May 16, 1933.

———. "Heavy Hail, Lightning Reported Near Enfield." July 12, 1938.

Springfield (MA) Republican. "Boston Arranges to Acquire Town for Water Supply." June 27, 1929.

———. "Boston's Plan to Take Swift River Water to Be Pressed in 1922." January 28, 1921.

———. "Death of a Prominent Enfield Man." April 19, 1902.

———. "Hold Dedication: Enfield Exercises at Soldiers' Monument." July 4, 1916.

———. "Enfield Folk Fear-Ridden Following Incendiary Fires." August 2, 1936.

———. "Enfield's History Ends." April 28, 1938.

———. "Enfield 100th Anniversary." March 18, 1916.

———. "Enfield Post Office Ends 116 Years." January 15, 1939.

———. "Enfield Ready for Centennial." July 1, 1916.

———. "Enfield Will Hold Farewell Ball and Reunion Tomorrow." April 26, 1938.

———. "Fifteen Men Killed: Only Portions of Their Bodies Could Be Found." January 23, 1910.

———. "Fireman's Ball Town's Final Social Event." April 16, 1938.

———. "Host of Swift River Valley Dead Is Gathering at Quabbin Park." February 5, 1933.

———. "Hundreds Attend Hearing in Town Hall at Enfield." May 5, 1922.

———. "Into the Valley of the Swift River Come 3,000 Men with Ax, Saw and Brush Hooks: Workers Start Clearing Land Preparing for the Lake That Will Flood the Area." June 7, 1936.

———. "New York Water Works: Villages Farms and Cemeteries Go to Make Way for the Reservoir." December 23, 1910.

———. "Old Enfield Church Marks 150th Anniversary Despite the Fact That Building Gone." August 10, 1936.

———. "Old Mill at Smith's Passing into History." July 20, 1930.

———. "Old Swift River Hotel at Enfield Being Torn Down." November 14, 1937.

———. "Quabbin Park." February 5, 1933.

———. "Sharp Attacks on Senate Water Supply Measure." May 21, 1926.

———. "Swift River Plant Sold." January 17, 1913.

———. "Swift River Valley Lives in Suspense Awaiting Flood of Rushing Waters." June 20, 1926.

———. "Town Centennial: Enfield's First Day." July 3, 1916.

———. "Voice Strong Opposition to Swift River Diversion." May 4, 1922.

Springfield (MA) Union. "Searchlight: The Longest Tunnel in the World." March 12, 1914.

———. "The Doctor." *Letters from Quabbin* 27, July 12, 1938.

———. "The Postmaster." *Letters from Quabbin* 26, July 7, 1938.

———. "The Quabbin Club." *Letters from Quabbin* 10, May 17, 1938.

Theroux, Gene (Geneht). "Enfield Gala Theatre V1 Part 1 24 Oct." https://www.youtube.com/watch?v=UvAJtqFZP-c.

Ware (MA) River News. "$5000 Bequest of Miss Marion A. Smith Used to Secure X-Ray Equipment." September 26, 1946.

———. "Antique Buyers from All Over New England Expected at Smith Auction." September 26, 1945.

———. "Enfield." 1908. Clipping from the collection of the Swift River Valley Historical Society.

———. "Gov. Curley Controls Picking 1300 Men to Clear Reservoir." April 29, 1936.

———. "Late Miss Marion Smith Left Well Over One Million Dollars." December 8, 1944.

———. "Leaves Generous Bequests to Scores of Friends and Charities." November 16, 1944.

———. "Miss Marion A. Smith Passes Away Here: Miss Marion Andrews Died at Her Beautiful Home on Highland Street Monday." November 8, 1944.

———. "Miss Smith of Enfield to Build Fine Home Here." Undated clipping from the collection of the Massachusetts Department of Conservation and Recreation.

———. "Notable Tribute Paid Enfield's Dr. Segur." January 30, 1939.

———. "Smith Auction Highly Successful in Spite of Stormy Weather." October 1945.

———. "Trying to Find More Work for Project Boys." September 30, 1936.

"Woman's Club…Quabbin Club Ends Career After Fort Fruitful Years." April 24, 1938. Clipping in the Enfield (MA) Collection at the University of Massachusetts's Robert S. Cox Special Collections & University Archives Research Center.

Worcester (MA) Gazette. "Ware Area Prices Are Under Inquiry." May 8, 1936.

———. "Ware Officials Deny Boosts in Food Costs." May 8, 1936.

Worcester (MA) Telegram. "1000 Still Working in Quabbin Area." December 8, 1936.

ABOUT THE AUTHOR

Elena Palladino grew up in Sturbridge, Massachusetts, and now lives with her family in Marion Smith's former home in Ware. She holds a BA in English from Simmons University, an MA in literary and cultural studies from Carnegie Mellon University and an EdM in higher education from Harvard University. She works in higher education in western Massachusetts. This is her first book.

For more information or to connect with Elena, visit https://QuabbinHouse.com or @QuabbinHouse on social media.